Hearing God's Voice

How Hearing God Will Cause You to Live Victoriously

By:
Kehinde Adesina

Copyright © 2010 Kehinde Adesina

Published 2013

All rights reserved. Any unauthorized broadcasting, public performance, copying or recording will constitute an infringement of copyright. Permission granted to reproduce for personal and educational use only. Commercial copying, hiring, lending is prohibited.

This work is registered with the UK Copyright Service.

ISBN: 978-1-909787-23-0

Published by Purpose2Destiny TK Limited

All scripture quotations are taken from the New King James Version (NKJV) unless otherwise indicated.

Other scriptures used are The New International Version (NIV) and The Amplified Bible (AMP)

(Small letter "s" is used in satan and not capitalized so as not to glorify him)

Dedication

To my Most Righteous God and Father who drew my ears and heart towards You to listen to Your voice so that I can hear the words pertaining to my life. If You had not drawn me towards You I would have gone amiss.

Acknowledgement

I thank my brother, Pastor Adebowale Adesina for his encouragement, insight, input and guidance given to me during the completion of this book and Georgina Chong-You for editing this book. I further thank Jumoke Ademola of Gemsjummy Photography who took the photo for the back cover of this book.

Table of Contents

Introduction	1
Chapter 1 – Do You Hear God's Voice?	5
Chapter 2 – Jesus Speaks Through The Ages	27
Chapter 3 – The Voice of The Holy Spirit	37
Chapter 4 – Praise, Worship & God	53
Chapter 5 – The Voice Of Wisdom	59
Chapter 6 – God Drowns Out the Enemy	69
Chapter 7 – God's Word Manifested in Season	81
Chapter 8 – Obstacles & Consequences of Failing to Hear God's Voice	101
Chapter 9 – The Importance of Hearing God's Voice	125
Conclusion	135

Introduction

This book is about hearing God speak to us. There is a hunger and desire in us all to hear directly from God concerning His plan and purpose for our lives. It is this desire in some that make them seek spiritual guidance through mediums and become embroiled in occult activities in their quest to converse and commune with a higher being. We must seek God alone and no other to reveal His plans to us. We must ask God to speak to us and wait to listen to what He has to say. Irrespective of the dawn that you are in, you must incline your ear to hear what God is saying to you as God says that He will be heard by those who call out to Him.

The ability to recognise God's voice comes with experience and time spent in His presence. In this life's busyness it becomes imperative that you **train your spiritual ears to hear God clearly and your spiritual eyes to see what God is showing you (Job 42:5)**. God speaks in different and diverse ways, which we cannot fathom. His methods are unique. Whatever word is spoken must correspond with the Bible, if it does not, then it is not from God.

All Christians hear God but often times most do not recognise that it is God speaking to them. We must learn to recognise His leadings, promptings and nudges. We must continue to develop our relationship with Him so that we can know when

He is speaking to us. We must not only read the Word, we must also listen to and hear what God is saying about each Word we receive.

Do you often wonder why some people remain calm in times of trouble? Why they go through life as if they face no challenges like others? Why they glide through trying times without being burnt? There is no mystery to this; it is simply because they have learnt how to recognise God's voice and trust in Him.

Does God still speak today? Does God speak only to a selected few or just to the prophets as He did in the days gone by or can He still be heard to speak to all those who believe in Him? Through our faith in Jesus Christ, we can certainly hear the Voice of God through the Holy Spirit who now dwells within us. We too are Priests unto our God to reign over the earth as God's ambassadors. God wants to commune with you and to have a relationship with you. You must cultivate and develop your relationship with Him.

The Church of God needs to hear God's voice if it is to become a voice to the Nations. The leaders, pastors, and ministers of God will only be able to move the Church of God forward if they individually and collectively incline their ears to hear what God is saying to the Church. Without God as the Head of the Church, there will be no growth in the lives of the believers the Church is professing to represent. God speaks to us so that we can serve His church and be a blessing to others.

Hearing God's voice is one thing, obeying His instructions is yet another matter. Obedience to God's Word is the key to success in life – it is better than sacrifice. Our obedience shows our heartfelt devotion and commitment to God and His Son, Jesus Christ, who sacrificed His life for us. Jesus Christ said that He and His Father (God) are One. You therefore need to hear Jesus Christ

Introduction

speak to you through His Holy Spirit if you are to follow the Will of God for your life.

I hope that as you begin to read through the chapters of this book that you will open up your heart, mind and soul to hear the message that God intends for you to receive. You must understand that all the scriptures in the Bible are inspired by God – "For the word of God is alive and active. Sharper than any double-edged sword, it penetrates even to dividing soul and spirit, joints and marrow; it judges the thoughts and attitudes of the heart" (Hebrews 4:12 NIV). Allow His words to penetrate your inner recesses, where men cannot reach and see God prove Himself mighty in your life.

CHAPTER 1

Do You Hear God's Voice?

Before you speak, it is necessary for you to listen, for God speaks in the silence of the heart. —Mother Teresa

God speaks. Do you hear God's voice when He speaks to you? It is crucial that you hear God when he speaks to you as His Words are active, operative and effective. A Word from God is all that you need to be a winner in life. God does not have to speak too many words before they are backed by power. Your life is of concern to God — anything that concerns you, automatically concerns Him. God will speak to defend your cause, to promote you and to manifest His Glory in your life. God speaks through His Holy Word, through circumstances that you may be facing, through His Prophets and sometimes through those around you.

> *The self-appointed spokesmen for God incline to shout; He, Himself, speaks only in whispers. —Martin H. Fischer*

Are you patient enough to hear His voice? In the commotion around you whose voice do you hear? Is it satan's or God's voice? You may sometimes feel confused because of the many voices vying for your attention, just keep tuning your ear to hear what God is saying and you will hear Him clearly. The devil may want to torment you into giving up, don't give up, and just hold on to God's word as He will speak to you during these challenging times. Don't allow the enemies' voice stop you from grasping hold of your victory.

God will not keep silent concerning your life; He will converse with you about the direction you should take as you journey through life. God has promised that He would not keep silent for your sake until your righteousness flows through and your victory is gained. He expects you to communicate regularly with Him and have a two-way conversation.

Two-Way Conversation:

Prayer is a two-way conversation. A two-way conversation is communication. As Christians we should not only talk (pray) to God but we must also position ourselves in such a way that we can listen to Him (John 8:47). Make sure that you keep silent long enough to hear what God is saying to you. After hearing what God says to you, you should do what He says you should do or refrain from doing what He says you shouldn't do. There is no benefit in hearing God for the sake of hearing as you must benefit from the word received. Do not harden your heart when you hear His voice so that you can enter His rest and be at peace.

God will provide solutions to your challenges when you call out to Him. Don't wallow in agony when you should be voicing your complaints to Him. God is always on-line and available; He will not disconnect your call or terminate your conversation with Him. Your role is to keep an open line with Him, as communication is crucial to keeping your momentum in life.

God Speaks – He is saying "We Need To Talk"

Speaking is God's Way of communicating with us. God not only speaks but He talks to us as well. He talks to us daily, continuously and regularly. We need God's revelation, insight and knowledge, not information overload which we often get from others. Whilst there is nothing wrong in watching Christian channels, reading Christian literatures or relying on the messages from the pulpit, we equally need to hear God confirm the word that we have received. You need God to reveal His Word to you in a manner that you will understand. You need to be attentive to God for He is saying "We need to Talk" - about your challenges, struggles and you. God might even need to talk to you about a loved one - sometimes God talks to you about someone close to you who is far away from home because He is concerned about them. What do you do when you receive this prompting from God? Do you ignore or act upon the prompting received? Don't forget that God is all knowing, seeing and hearing. There have been occasions when God has brought to my mind persons I have not seen in years. At these times, I know He wants me to either intercede, pray or to follow up on a call to them to enquire about their welfare.

How do you respond when you get a message, text or email from someone you love saying "we need to talk"? You are expectant, you wait for the clock to tick, and you count down the seconds, minutes, hours and perhaps days when you will next hear their voice. Your loved ones may be far away from home, and despite the time difference you are not mindful to wait up to take their call as you can't wait to hear from them again. When you have a personal relationship with God, you will want to resume your conversation with Him, no matter your schedule. God is waiting not only to speak but to talk with you today, what about you?

Recognising God's Voice:

You will only learn to recognise God's voice when your spirit is one with His as your spirit will be sensitive to His voice. You must develop an awareness of your inner spirit who will prompt you to be alert and sensitive to God. The reason why some cannot recognise or identify that it is God who is speaking to them is because they don't' have a close relationship with Him. His Spirit cannot commune with their spirit to ensure them of His presence resulting in the devil deceiving them.

When your parents, siblings or close friends call you on the phone, you immediately recognise their voice. You recognise their voice because of your closeness to them and have imprinted their voices on your mind; you also catch them out when they try to disguise their voices. So it is when you have a close relationship with God and are in constant communication with Him. You will know when He is the One speaking with you and when He is not. You must learn to distinguish God's voice from those of the enemy as counterfeits are rampant today.

The Significance of Hearing, Recognising & Obeying God's Voice from an early age:

The fact that you may be an adolescent is not a bar to hearing from God. You must learn to recognise, heed and obey God when He speaks to you. **You must not say to yourself that you are too young to hear from God. God wants to train your spiritual ears to hear Him speak to you.** As parents we must not say to ourselves that our children are too young to hear God. In Proverbs 22:6, we are told to train up our children in the way they should go so that when they grow up they would not depart from the training we have given them. We need to teach our children how to listen out for God and to obey His instructions. God spoke to children in the Bible notably Samuel amongst others, we can see in the lives of Samuel and King Josiah below that it is never too early to start hearing from God and obeying His Voice:-

- Samuel ministered to the Lord at a time when the Word of The Lord was rare and precious like gold. The Word of God had ceased as Eli, the Prophet was no longer receiving any revelation from The Lord as he had become lukewarm in his service to God. God called and spoke to Samuel revealing what His plans for Israel and for the household of Eli was. God chose Samuel at an early age to replace Eli as his successor *(1 Samuel 3)*. Samuel hearkened to God's voice and served God with the whole of his heart until his death.

- King Josiah was eight years old when he began his reign. In the 18th year of his reign, Hilkiah, the High Priest found the Book of the Law in the House of the Lord, Hilkiah gave it to Shapan, the Scribe who in turn gave it to King Josiah. When King Josiah realised the consequences of Israel's indifference and idolatry in not following God's Word, he tore his clothes in humility. He sent Hilkiah, the priest to Huldah, the prophetess to seek God's face and petition God on behalf of his people. Prophetess Huldah prophesied good tidings to King Josiah for honouring the Lord and repenting. The Bible records that there was no other king before or after King Josiah who turned to the Lord with all his heart, soul and might *(2 Kings 22)*.

I remember vividly an incident when I was in the fourth grade in secondary school. My father had told me one Sunday afternoon on our way home from church that he wanted me to change school. The new school being proposed was in another state of the country which involved a 2-3 hours journey by plane and which would involve me staying in a boarding house. I argued against my changing schools, saying I was not going. When we were about ten minutes from home, I heard the voice of God telling me clearly that my time for change had come and that for me to fully live and fulfil my potential I had to leave my family, friends and present location. I suddenly became quiet and stopped arguing with my father in the car. When we got home, I informed my father that I was now happy to change school and I asked him when I would be leaving home. I went to my room to begin packing my bags straight away. My parents looked at each other as they were shocked by my sudden change of heart; they thought I must have had a brain wave!

The following week I left for boarding school and within four months I gave my life to Jesus Christ. I become serious about my schooling and God's plan for my life suddenly became clearer. Had I not heard God and obeyed His voice, the course of my life would have fundamentally changed as I would have failed my GCSE's and would have become a lost cause. During this same period, God told me that He wanted me to spend my break time studying rather than playing. I obeyed God's instructions and started attending the library each break time. This habit of studying enabled me develop the ability to be focussed, a skill which I later required when I became a lawyer in later years.

The Significance of Hearing, Recognising & Obeying God's Voice in your mature years:

Aging should not be a bar to hearing from God, it does not matter whether you are middle aged or of retirement age, you must learn to recognise God's Voice at each stage of your growth so that God can direct your path as you live out your days. Those who hear from God will live according to His standard and not according to the world's or dictates of men.

- God spoke to Abraham when he was 99 years old to circumcise himself and his household in readiness of His Promises (Genesis 17). Abraham acted on God's Word and was blessed.

- God appeared to Jacob when he was 130 years old, He told Jacob not to be afraid to go down to Egypt to join Joseph (Genesis 46: 1-3). Jacob heeded God's voice and lived out the rest of his days in peace.

It is evident that Christians can only attain spiritual maturity and live successfully when they hear God's voice. God speaks to the inner man thorough His spirit and changes Man from within. The Old and New Testament detail numerous persons who heard the Voice of God and by their doing so they changed the course of their lives. God started to speak from the beginning of creation in the Book of Genesis all through to the final chapters of the Book of Revelation.

In the Old testament God spoke to our forefathers through the prophets, through Angels, in dreams and in Visions. God spoke to Joseph and Daniel in dreams; Abraham in a vision; the birth of Samson was announced to his mother by an Angel; He spoke to Elijah in a whisper; Job was spoken to in a storm and Balaam through his donkey. He spoke when He rebuked the children of Israel for their disobedience, when He provided Moses with the Ten Commandments and when He wanted to bless the children of Israel.

In the New testament God speaks to us by his Son (Jesus Christ), whom He appointed heir of all things, and through whom He made the universe. Whilst Jesus was on earth He walked in complete obedience to God because He heard His father's voice clearly. He received God's direction through His Spirit. Jesus described Himself as the true shepherd and His followers His sheep, He stated that His sheep knows His voice and listens to His voice. Jesus promised to manifest Himself to those who keep His commandments.

God has always spoken and He still speaks. God speaks to us when He approves or disapproves of our behaviour. He speaks to punish our enemies, invoke a blessing on us or rebuke us for our sins. He will speak to admonish, warn, teach and train you just as He did with Moses and the Prophets. God promises to be your God when you obey His commandments and walk in His ways. The Bible says that:-

God Spoke at Creation -

> *Yes, My hand has laid the foundation of the earth, and My right hand has spread out the heavens; when I call to them, they stand forth together [to execute My decrees] Isaiah 48: 13 (Amp).*

Creation is God's Word manifested. God noticed the state of the universe so He spoke up for change; He had seen that the earth was without form, empty and void. By His Word He called the Heavens, Earth and every living thing into existence. He commanded light to show its face and separate itself from darkness and it did. Then He called light day, and called the darkness night. God needed light so that all that came afterwards could be seen.

God commanded the firmament to be separated from the waters, which He called the Heavens. He spoke to the waters to be gathered together to make room for dry land and they obeyed His voice. God called the dry land Earth and the waters Seas. God looked at what He had created and was satisfied with His Handiwork. He then ordered the earth to produce all types of vegetation, seeds and fruits according to their kind and they obeyed His Voice. God wasn't tired of speaking for He knew that the Essence of Life was in His mouth. He spoke into existence the days, months and years. He made two great lights, the greater He called the sun to govern the affairs of the day, and the lesser He called the moon to govern the affairs of the night.

He spoke to the waters to bring forth moving creatures and the Heavens to bring forth birds. He created the great sea monsters and every living creature that moves and every winged bird according to its kind. God blessed His creation and told them to be fruitful and to multiply. He pronounced an irrevocable blessing on them and they have not ceased abiding according to His pronouncement (Genesis 1:21-22).

He also created man by the words of His mouth. He then sealed His irrevocable covenant with man by no other name than Himself. You too must speak into existence that which has not yet manifested itself in the physical realm. **Your positive confession will bring into manifestation the things that are unseen.** Even if they do not already exist, God will honour your words when you speak out in faith. Just as God spoke up for creation you too must be bold and speak out in faith. God wants you to open your mouth wide so that He can fill them up with good things (Psalms 81:10).

God has declared your end from the beginning and His prophecy to you will come to pass. His mercy, love and faithfulness continue through all generations. *He declared in Isaiah 46: 10 (NIV) that, "I make known the end from the beginning, from ancient* times, what is still to come. I say: *My purpose will stand, and I will do all that I please.*" Just as He has decreed concerning you, so will it be. **Even in the hustle and bustle of your life you must call upon God and He will give you a word for each moment.**

God Speaks Against Those Who Dishonour His Name -

God requires that His Name is revered and honoured above every other name. He despises those who wilfully disobey His instructions and bring His Name into disrepute. God will not permit you to magnify anything above Him, as He is a jealous God who will not share His glory with another.

God repeatedly sent His prophets to the Israelites to warn them about their debase behaviour but they ignored the prophets and continued in their folly. They profaned His Name in the manner of their worship so He punished them for their sins. The Israelites had deceived themselves that they were untouchable by reason of the covenant God had with their forefathers. You must not provoke God to the extent that all your good deeds are nullified before Him.

When Aaron's sons, Nadab and Abihu dishonoured God by offering a strange and unholy fire before Him, He killed them. When God gives His instructions for worship, He expects us to abide by them. When we dishonour Him in worship He will reprove and rebuke us as He deems fit. We can either take His corrections in a mature manner or arrogantly refuse to listen to Him and be punished for our disobedience (Leviticus 10:1-3). We've seen examples where God has allowed terror and calamity to befall those who spurn His instructions. He humbled the Israelites' pride when they arrogantly stood against Him and made the Heavens as brass to them as punishment for their disobedience.

When Sennacherib, King of Assyria sent a threatening letter through the hands of his messengers to King Hezekiah that he was going to destroy him and his supporters, King Hezekiah went to the Lord in prayer, asking God to open His ears to hear all the words spoken against His Name in contempt and derision. The Lord responded by sending a message to Sennacherib that no one had ever mocked, discredited, insulted or blasphemed the Almighty God of Israel and got away with it. **God will not share or give His glory to another by permitting your enemies to triumph over you. He will stand up to defend His Holy Name.**

> *"This is the word which the Lord has spoken concerning him: The Virgin Daughter of Zion has despised you and laughed you to scorn; the Daughter of Jerusalem has shaken her head behind you. Whom have you mocked and reviled [insulted and blasphemed]? And against Whom have you raised your voice and haughtily lifted your eyes? Against the Holy One of Israel! By your servants you have mocked, reproached, insulted, and defied the Lord, and you have said, With my many chariots I have gone up to the height of the mountains, to the inner recesses of Lebanon... [But, says the God of Israel] have you not heard that I purposed to do it long ago, that I planned it in ancient times? Now I have brought it to pass, that you [king of Assyria] should [be My instrument to] lay waste fortified cities, making them ruinous heaps...But I [the Lord] know your sitting down and your going out and your coming in and your raging against Me. Because your raging against Me and your arrogance and careless ease have come to My ears, therefore will I put My hook in your nose and My bridle in your lips, and I will turn you back by the way you came. Isaiah 37:22-29 (Amp).*

God Speaks To Bless You -

God speaks when He wants to bless you. Your duty is to pay attention when He speaks so that you can **receive all that He has in store for you**. God will always hear your voice provided you listen to and obey His instructions. God will bless you beyond your wildest imagination even when you think you are out of reach or out of sight.

God visited Noah and his family after the flood and established His covenant with his descendants and swore never to destroy man again (Genesis 8). God spoke with Abram when He wanted to bless him. He asked Abram to leave his people and go to a place that He had prepared for him. God promised to bless Abram's descendants and make them immeasurable like the sands of the earth and He changed Abram's name to Abraham and his wife's name to Sarah as a seal of His covenant and blessings.

God will find you as He did with Haggai and Ishmael whose cry for help came up to Him in Heaven out of the wilderness of Beersheba. God promised to provide comfort and shelter to Haggai and Ishmael during their sojourn in the wilderness and to meet their every need. He promised to perpetually bless Ishmael and his descendants forever (Genesis 21:17-20).

God told Isaac whilst he dwelt in Gerar during the time of famine not to uproot himself and go down to Egypt. He promised to bless and favour him as He had done with his father, Abraham, before him provided he was obedient to His charge, commandments, statute and laws. Because Isaac obeyed God, he reaped a hundredfold return on his harvest that year (Genesis 26:2-6). There is a marked difference between those who wait on God before they act and those who go out on their own.

God spoke to Jacob on numerous occasions in his dreams: He informed Jacob that his destiny and location in life will change. He changed Jacob's name to Israel as a seal of His promise. God still speaks through visions of the night, when the mind and spirit is at rest. Ask God to speak to you like He has never done before, so that you can receive a fresh revelation of Him.

God Speaks When You Mistrust Him -

Whilst Moses was up on the mountain speaking with God, the Israelites got Aaron to make a graven image for them as they felt Moses was taking too long with God. This displeased God as it showed their distrust of him. They misinterpreted Moses' delay as God's inability to fulfil His promises to them. Although Moses was still on the mountain, God told him what the Israelites were doing in his absence. God was angry that the Israelites had quickly forgotten how He had delivered them out of Egypt so He wanted to destroy them but Moses petitioned God on their behalf for mercy (Exodus 32: 7-14).

God spoke against Saul for his unwillingness to trust Him. Although He initially spoke up for Saul's promotion as king over Israel, He later demoted Saul for his arrogance and disobedience. When Samuel wept for Saul, God reprimanded him for weeping and mourning for the person whom He had rejected (1 Samuel 15).

God Speaks When You are Mistreated by Others -

God always speaks up for us when we are mistreated by others. God says He defends the defenceless. He will not keep quiet when we are being taken advantage of. He intervened on behalf of the

Israelite women whose husbands were marrying and divorcing them at will for no cogent reason, but to satisfy their own carnal desires. God noticed that the men came to the temple to worship Him but that their hearts were not right so He reprimanded them by telling them their worship was abhorrent and contemptible to Him. You cannot mistreat your wife/husband, partner, siblings, parents or relatives during the week and go to church on Sunday in feigned piety. **God sees, knows and hears all things and your actions are not hidden from Him.** Shouting and praying to God is futile when you have mistreated your nearest and dearest. God would prefer that you get up from your knees and go home and shed a tear of shame for your behaviour than remain in His presence.

> *And this is the second thing you do: You cover the altar of the LORD with tears, With weeping and crying; So He does not regard the offering anymore, Nor receive it with goodwill from your hands. Yet you say, "For what reason?" Because the LORD has been witness between you and the wife of your youth; With whom you have dealt treacherously; Yet she is your companion And your wife by covenant. ... Therefore take heed to your spirit, and let none deal treacherously with the wife of his youth. " For the LORD God of Israel says That He hates divorce, For it covers one's garment with violence," ... Malachi 2: 13-16*

In Exodus 3 we read that God spoke with Moses about the mistreatment of His people (Israel) in Egypt. He told Moses that He had seen the affliction of His people and He had heard their cries from His Holy hill. He sent Moses to deliver His people out of the hands of Pharaoh and to take them out of bondage, enslavement and captivity. Although Pharaoh initially refused to comply with God's message to let His people go, when God destroyed every first born of Egypt from humans to animals, pharaoh understood that there was no God equal to the living God of Israel. Your enemy might think that they can pursue and overtake you but God will deliver you from their clutches. He will destroy the untouchables who have only an earthly influence.

When Aaron and Miriam spoke against Moses, God heard their grumblings; He punished Miriam by bringing leprosy upon her and spared Aaron because of the Priesthood which would have excluded him from service. God informed them that whilst He spoke with other prophets and many others in parables and prophesies He spoke with Moses directly mouth-to-mouth and face-to-face (meaning Moses saw God's presence). God called Moses His friend, with whom He conversed (Numbers 12).

The Lord also rebuked David for sleeping with Bathsheba, Uriah's wife and for murdering Uriah to cover up his adultery. God said that the sword will never depart from David's house and that his neighbour would sleep with his wives in the sight of the sun (i.e. in full view of the public). God told David that he would be judged openly for what he had done in secret. **Hidden sins are not really hidden before God, who sees all and knows all things** (II Samuel: 12).

God Speaks To Defend You From Your Enemies -

God says that because you are the apple or pupil of His eyes anyone who touches you pokes their hands in His eyes. He will not keep silent when He knows that you have been troubled. He would vent His anger against those who waive their hands at you in derision or looks at you haughtily. God will deal with those who challenge you and He will rebuke them for your sake. **God says that He would plunder your enemies who have plundered you in the past;** He will rebuke satan on your behalf.

We know the story of Abram, whilst in Egypt, who deceived Pharaoh, about his relationship with Sarai but still God spoke to Pharaoh not to touch Sarai and He brought plagues upon the land on account of Abram (Genesis 12:14-20). The same scenario happened when Abimelech, King of Gerar took Sarai as his wife, God warned Abimelech not to touch her and to hand her back to Abram. God was still Abram's shield, protector and defender despite his deceit; He rose up to protect Abram because of the covenant He had made with him (Genesis 20).

We also know the story of Cain who killed Abel, his brother. Abel's voice cried to the Lord in anguish for vindication causing God to rise up from His Judgement Seat. Although Cain denied any wrongdoing and stated that he did not know where Abel was, God had seen everything and heard every word spoken by Cain in anger and resentment. When you stay close to God, He will surround you with His arms and cover you with His garment to shield you from the evil attack of your enemies. King David said that when his enemies and foes came up against him, they stumbled and fell and that even when a thousand hosts were encamped around against him, his heart did not fear because he knew that his confidence was in God who had spoken with him to assure him of victory at all times (Psalms 27:2-3).

When you are weak and weary God will raise you up. Cry out to the Lord for help in times of trouble and He will vindicate you.

> "And Jacob outwitted Laban the Syrian [Aramean] in that he did not tell him that he [intended] to flee and slip away secretly. So he fled with all that he had, ... But on the third day Laban was told that Jacob had fled. So he took his kinsmen with him and pursued after [Jacob] for seven days... But God came to Laban the Syrian [Aramean]

> *in a dream by night and said to him, Be careful that you do not speak from good to bad to Jacob [peaceably, then violently]. Then Laban overtook Jacob... And Laban said to Jacob, What do you mean stealing away and leaving like this without my knowing it, and carrying off my daughters as if captives of the sword? Why did you flee secretly and cheat me and did not tell me, ... It is in my power to do you harm; but the God of your father spoke to me last night, saying, Be careful that you do not speak from good to bad to Jacob [peaceably, then violently]. Genesis 31:20-29 (Amp)*

The Bible passage above clearly shows how God rose up for Jacob and fought his corner by warning Laban not to cause any harm to Jacob resulting in his safety.

Korah, Dathan and Abiram rose up with On, 150 princes and some elders of Israel against Moses by questioning his authority to lead them. When God heard their dissension He punished them by sending fire into their tents to devour them and their supporters. When the people of Israel complained about their death, God wanted to kill them all but Moses interceded on their behalf to stop the plague that had begun in their midst. Likewise Numbers 22 tells us that when Balak, the King of Moab saw how Israel had dealt with the Amorites, he sent for Balaam, a sorcerer to curse Israel, however on his way, God rebuked Balaam through his donkey which spoke with a human voice to curtail his movement. God took over Balaam's vocal chords so that he could pronounce only blessings on them instead of a curse.

> *The utterance of him who hears the words of God, Who sees the vision of the Almighty, Who falls down, with eyes wide open: "How lovely are your tents, O Jacob! Your dwellings, O Israel! ... "His king shall be higher than Agag, And his kingdom shall be exalted... He shall consume the nations,*

> his enemies; He shall break their bones And pierce them with his arrows. 'He bows down, he lies down as a lion; And as a lion, who shall rouse him?' "Blessed is he who blesses you, And cursed is he who curses you. Then Balak's anger was aroused against Balaam, and he struck his hands together; and Balak said to Balaam, "I called you to curse my enemies, and look, you have bountifully blessed them these three times! Now therefore, flee to your place. I said I would greatly honour you, but in fact, the LORD has kept you back from honour."" Numbers 24: 4-11

Anyone who tries to tamper with your destiny will find their end to be like that of the Moabites. God has sworn by Himself that it shall be well with you and **His promises cannot be revoked by your enemies, who hire agents of darkness to curse your future. Their curses will have no effect on you.** The Lord will assign angels to destroy all those who rise up against you and give you victory. When Joshua was close to entering Jericho, he looked up and saw a man who had drawn His sword. Joshua enquired if He was with Israel or against them. The man replied neither but that He was there as the Prince of the Lord's Host. He was on assignment to defeat Israel's enemies. God will rise up at the right time to deliver you out of your enemy's hands (Joshua 5: 13-14).

When the Prophets of Baal began to dominate the religious climate and instil fear in the obedient servants of God during the days of Elijah, Elijah called them to a meeting at Mount Carmel to determine once and for all whose God was the most powerful. He told them to call upon their gods and he would call upon his God and the One who answered by fire was the true and living God. It was no surprise that the false gods remained mute but God heard Elijah's voice and brought an all-consuming fire to fall upon his burnt sacrifice. God answered Elijah by fire to vindicate him before the false prophets and gods. When the people saw what happened they fell on their faces and said that the Lord "He is God" (1 Kings 18:20-39).

The above testimonies give us assurance that God not only speaks to His children but He will speak up and fight for us. Never hesitate on calling on Him for help for He will certainly deliver you out of trouble.

> *I found this anonymous inspired message about calling on God, it provides scriptures that believers can rely upon when they are facing challenges and wish to hear from God urgently. It is entitled "emergency telephone numbers" it states that the numbers are more effective than 911 (USA), (999) United Kingdom. You may insert your own country's emergency number, whatever that might be!*

These are more effective than 911 (999) numbers that you make to earth's emergency services.

Emergency	Telephone Numbers
When	
You are sad, phone:	John 14
You have sinned, phone:	Psalm 51
You are facing danger, phone:	Psalm 91
People have failed you, phone:	Psalm 27
It feels as though God is far from you, phone:	Psalm 139
Your faith needs stimulation, phone:	Hebrews 11
You are alone and scared, phone:	Psalm 23
You are worried, phone:	Matthew: 8:19-34
You are hurt and critical, phone:	1 Corinthians 13
You wonder about Christianity, phone:	2 Corinthians 5:15-18
You feel like an outcast, phone:	Romans 8:31-39

Hearing God's Voice

You are seeking peace, phone:	Matthew 11: 25-30
It feels as if the world is bigger than God, phone:	Psalm 90
You need Christ like insurance, phone:	Romans 8:1-30
You are leaving home for a trip, phone:	Psalm 121
You are praying for yourself, phone:	Psalm 87
You require courage for a task, phone:	Joshua 1
Inflation's and investments are hogging your thoughts, phone:	Mark 10:17-31
You are depressive, phone:	Psalm: 27
Your bank account is empty, phone:	Psalm: 37
You lose faith in mankind, phone;	1 Corinthians 13
It looks like people are unfriendly, phone:	John 15
You are losing hope, phone:	Psalm 126
You feel the world is small compared to you, phone:	Psalm 19
You want to carry fruit, phone:	John: 15
/Paul's secret for happiness, phone:	Colossians 3:12-17
With big opportunity/ discovery, phone:	Isaiah: 55
To get along with other people, phone:	Romans 12
ALTERNATE	**NUMBERS**
For dealing with fear, call:	Psalm 47
For security, call:	Psalm 121: 3
For assurance, call:	Mark 8:35
For reassurance, call:	Psalm 145:18

ALL THESE NUMBERS MAY BE PHONED DIRECTLY. NO OPERATOR ASSISTANCE IS NECESSARY. ALL LINES TO HEAVEN ARE AVAILABLE 24 HOURS A DAY. FEED YOUR FAITH, AND DOUBT WILL STARVE TO DEATH.

My prayer for you is that you will hear God clearly when He speaks to you, as His Words will soothe, comfort and uphold you. God's Word will also change your life for the best and it will keep you on track.

CHAPTER 2

Jesus Speaks Through The Ages

"IN THE beginning [before all time] was the Word (Christ), and the Word was with God, and the Word was God Himself. He was present originally with God. All things were made and came into existence through Him; and without Him was not even one thing made that has come into being. In Him was Life, and the Life was the Light of men" —John 1: 1-4 (Amp).

The Gospel of John makes us understand that from the onset, at the very beginning, before all time Jesus Christ existed. Jesus was present with God before the foundation of the world, in Him was Life and this "Life" was the Light of men. He is the Invisible God, He is One with God. He is the Word, the Essence of Life, the Lamb of God, the Giver and Provider of our Salvation. His Voice was heard in the ages past and His Voice can still be heard in this age.

> *Jesus can be heard by all who call upon Him. Jesus speaks to call us to Himself as He desires that we have an intimate relationship with Him. He calls those who are weary to come to Him so that they can find rest.*

The Bible records the message, ministry and miracles of Jesus Christ. It gives great examples of Jesus Christ speaking out and becoming personally involved in the wellbeing of his followers to their betterment. Anytime Jesus gets involved in our lives, real changes begin to happen. The Bible states that:-

Jesus Spoke To Command Changes In Peoples Lives -

Jesus Christ spoke to bring a turnaround in the spiritual, emotional, physical, mental and financial lives of the people He came across. When Jesus spoke whatever was holding the people captive let go of them because of the power in Him. In some instances, the people acted in faith on hearing His Words and they received their miracle. John 2:1-11 states that Jesus Christ stepped into a precarious situation to rescue the bridegroom from embarrassment when the wine had run out at the wedding party. Jesus asked the servants to fill water pots with water and to draw some of it out. When they drew the water out they discovered that it had turned into wine- water came alive to the sound of His Voice and did His bidding.

On another occasion, when the multitude that came out to hear Jesus speak became hungry; Jesus gave thanks to God for the little food His disciples had gathered up. He blessed the food, which increased to fill the hunger of the crowd- the food heard, recognised and obeyed His voice. They took on a life of their own obeying the living Word of God. John 11 states that Jesus restored Lazarus back to life, his spirit which had long departed obeyed Jesus' voice and returned into him.

Matthew 8 records some of Jesus Christ's works. In Matthew 8: 1-3, we read that Jesus commanded a leper to be cleansed. Jesus was willing to see the man healed of his leprosy instead of remaining in the dregs of life and in despair. The man's healing was obvious for everyone to see. After this He went on to heal the centurion's servant who was sick far away at home, the servant recovered from the sickness at the exact moment Jesus spoke a Word of command. The scripture says that:

> "Now when Jesus had entered Capernaum, a centurion came to Him, pleading with Him, saying, "Lord, my servant is lying at home paralyzed, dreadfully tormented." And Jesus said to him, "I will come and heal him." The centurion answered and said, "Lord, I am not worthy that You should come under my roof. But only speak a word, and my servant will be healed. For I also am a man under authority, having soldiers under me. And I say to this one, 'Go,' and he goes; and to another, 'Come,' and he comes; and to my servant, 'Do this,' and he does it." When Jesus heard it, He marvelled, and said to those who followed, "Assuredly, I say to you, I have not found such great faith, not even in Israel! And I say to you that many will come from east and west, and sit down with Abraham, Isaac, and Jacob in the kingdom of heaven. But the sons of the kingdom will be cast out into outer darkness. There will be weeping and gnashing of teeth." Then Jesus said to the centurion, "Go your way; and as you have believed, so let it be done for you." And his servant was healed that same hour (Matthew 8: 5-13).

Matthew 8:16 (NIV) records that on the same day Jesus healed many people who had various ailments and who were under the power of demons. He restored all of them to health by the utterances of His mouth. It states that, *"When evening had come, they brought to Him many who were demon-possessed. And He cast out the spirits with a word, and healed all who were sick, that it might be fulfilled which was spoken by Isaiah the prophet, saying: He Himself took our infirmities And bore our sicknesses."*

In Matthew 8:23-27 Jesus spoke to instil peace into the troubled storm, which His disciples found themselves in. Jesus commanded the wind and the sea to keep their peace and they obeyed His voice. In Matthew 8:28-34 Jesus commanded the demons in the two men in the country of the Gadarenes to come out of them, at the sound of His voice, they loosened their control of these men.

As Jesus was going outside Jericho, two blind men sitting by the roadside called and cried out to Him to have mercy on them. Although they were silenced by the crowd, these two men kept shouting until Jesus heard them; Jesus granted them their request and immediately they regained their sight. Jesus stopped because He heard their cries for help (Matthew 20:29-34).

When Jesus hears your voice He will stop and respond.

The Gospel of Mark also records a number of Jesus' Works. Mark 5:25-34 states that Jesus healed the woman with the issue of blood who had been plagued by her condition for twelve years. He stopped to minister to her and He told the woman to take courage as He saw her faith to be healed. He went with Jarius to his house to resurrect his daughter who had died; at the sound of His voice the spirit of the girl, who had departed, returned back to her. In Mark 9:14-29, Jesus rebuked the demon that was tormenting a boy whom the disciples could not heal. He commanded the demon to come of the boy and the boy was healed.

Similarly Luke also records Jesus' Works, Luke 7:12-16 says that when Jesus touched the funeral bier of a young man who had died and was being carried by his family for burial, the man rose from death. It stated that Jesus commanded the man's spirit, which had departed to return into him and the spirit obeyed His Voice. The dead man rose to bring joy to his weeping mother. In Luke 13:11-13, Jesus healed the woman He saw in the Synagogue who had been bound for eighteen years. He spoke a word of faith to comfort her and the woman became whole; the sprit of infirmity holding her down loosened its grip over her.

You must always hear and follow the voice of the Good Shepherd. Jesus Christ is the True Shepherd who would lead you to safety. He willingly gave up His life for you so that you will be secured in Him. Your wholeness, security and safety is dependent upon your reliance on Jesus as your soul's necessity. He is the Good Shepherd of the fold. You must recognise and follow His voice because He has laid His life down to protect and preserve you. Jesus said that the sheep that belongs to Him will always hear and listen to His voice

> When you accept Jesus Christ into your heart you will stop searching for what is missing in your life. The emptiness, void and loneliness you feel will begin to dissipate.

and He will give them eternal life. Jesus has prayed in advance for your redemption and prosperity, don't take your salvation for granted (John 17: 15-24).

On my part, I have noticed my gradual dependence on Jesus alone. The emptiness in my life which I felt could not be filled by anyone has being filled by Him. Your reliance on Christ will make you a fulfilled person. Heed His voice as your soul's necessity, seek after Him and see the changes that will begin to take place. **Honour, revere and embrace Him and He will draw closer to you.**

Jesus Spoke Against The Evil Of His days and To Those Who Opposed His Ministry -

Jesus spoke against the cities of Chorazin, Bethsaida and Capernaum for trying to curtail and oppose His ministry. The people heard His message of repentance but closed their hearts to His words which could bring them redemption and forgiveness of sins (Matthew 11: 20-24). He rebuked the Pharisees who opposed His healing the sick on the Sabbath. He did not allow their criticism to prevent Him from doing the work God had sent Him to do. There will always be antagonists surrounding you who will never approve of the manner in which you carry out your God-given assignment. Nevertheless, **you must follow Jesus Christ's example and continue your mission.**

When the Pharisees tried to undermine Jesus' miracles by saying that He had healed a blind and dumb man by the power of Beelzebub, the prince of demons, He responded by telling them that the Kingdom of God had come upon them. He informed them that if they overstepped their boundary and spoke against the Holy Spirit of God, they will never be forgiven for their blasphemy or uncensored speech. He called them a brood of vipers and warned them they will be held accountable on the day of judgement for every word spoken by them in derision.

Mark 3:10-12 states that Jesus healed many people of their diseases so that on some occasions unclean spirits fell down before Him and kept screaming that He was the Son of God but He charged them strictly to remain silent. Jesus did not permit the demons to speak or reveal who He was because His mission on earth had not yet been accomplished. He did not want the unclean demons to sabotage His ministry of healing and restoring people back to their health.

When satan took Jesus Christ to the top of the mountain and showed Him all the kingdoms of the earth, which he boasted of owning, Jesus overcame satan by the words of His confessions. He told satan that the Authority, Power and Glory he spoke of did not belong to him but to God alone. He reminded satan that he did not have the legal basis to offer as a gift or for purchase, that which did not belong to him. A Latin maxim, which says **"Nemo dat** *quod non habet"*, **which** in English means "one cannot give what one does not have" held true in Jesus' time and still holds true today. **Satan cannot threaten you with adversity because he has no basis to do so without the permission of God or yourself.**

> "And the tempter came and said to Him, If You are God's Son, command these stones to be made loaves of]bread. But He replied, It has been written, Man shall not live and be upheld and sustained by bread alone, but by every word that comes forth from the mouth of God. Then the devil took Him into the holy city and placed Him on a turret (pinnacle, gable) of the temple sanctuary. And he said to Him, If You are the Son of God, throw Yourself down; for it is written, He will give His angels charge over you, and they will bear you up on their hands, lest you strike your foot against a stone. Jesus said to him, On the other hand, it is written also, You shall not tempt, test thoroughly, or try exceedingly the Lord your God. Again, the devil took Him up on a very high mountain and showed Him all the kingdoms of the world and the glory (the splendour, magnificence, pre-eminence, and excellence) of them. And he said to Him, These things, all taken together, I will give You, if You will prostrate Yourself before me and do homage and worship me. Then Jesus said to him, Be gone, Satan! For it has been written, You shall worship the Lord your God, and Him alone shall you serve" Mathew 4: 3-10 (Amp).

Jesus had clearly been communicating with His Father in Heaven so He knew which voice was original and which was a counterfeit. Because He knew His Father's voice He did not permit satan to distort who God had said He was. Sometimes words are spoken to you in the guise of spirituality which on the surface appears godly but when broken down are really destructive, deadly and demonic. You must speak out and take your stand against

Hearing God's Voice

these dream killers, thieves and polluters. As ministering angels are surrounding you to carry out your command, you must be careful not to affirm the negative, derogatory and unscriptural words pronounced upon you by others so that they don't become fulfilled. Hold on to the word God has placed in your heart.

Jesus accused the religious fanatics of trying to kill Him, He saw that they were spiritually deaf and blind as they did not receive any revelation at all of who He was, and neither did they receive His words, which could transform their lives. Because they could not understand Jesus, they accused Him of belonging to the devil and being possessed by him. He compared those who opposed Him to white washed tombs, which were full of dead bones and decay but outwardly, appeared beautiful. He told them that they will not escape eternal condemnation unless they repented of their sins. You must be careful how you speak out against others as your words will either justify and acquit you before God or condemn and sentence you for your ignorance.

Jesus also spoke out against the injustice of the Pharisees, Scribes and Sadducees who felt pure and holy in their own sight. He noticed that they burdened the Israelites with rules, doctrines and laws, which they themselves could not live by. Jesus called them pretenders and hypocrites who shut the Kingdom of Heaven in men's faces which they themselves did not seek to enter. He called them blind fools who were yokes on the people's necks as they refused to lighten their loads of spiritual bondage. Jesus wanted no gimmicks in His Temple; likewise in our lives He wants no more gimmicks taking place in our worship of God.

Jesus Speaks To Us Today -

Jesus assures us today that when we call upon Him He will keep His promises to us. He promised Peter the keys of the Kingdom of Heaven so that whatsoever Peter opened his mouth to bind as improper will be so bound and whatsoever he loosed by his mouth will be loosened by God in Heaven (Mathew 16:18-19). This scripture is also meant for the Believer today. Jesus expects us to call upon Him in faith for whatever we need. He assures us that whatever we bind on earth will be bound in Heaven and whatever we loose on earth would be loosed in heaven.

Jesus Christ, the mediator speaks on our behalf to God, our Father. His Blood, which He shed on Calvary, also speaks better things for us. You must not reject Jesus Christ's message of hope, mercy and restoration when you hear it being preached to you today (Hebrews 12: 24-25). **Jesus says that He stands at the door of your heart knocking for you to let Him in.** He says that if anyone hears, listens to, heeds His voice and opens the door for Him; He will come in and dine with that person. God desires that all men be saved from eternal commendation and spiritual death and live in the knowledge of Jesus Christ.

We have heard testimonies from believers of today about how Jesus has set them free to live a wholesome life, which proves to us that Christ is much alive and He can be heard to speak today as He did in the ages past. He is still with us today helping, restoring, protecting, delivering, equipping, guarding and keeping us for Himself until we meet Him face to face. He is very much with you today than ever before, we surely have a new hope in Christ. You must believe Him when He says that He will never leave you nor forsake you and that He will be with you until the end of time (Matthew 28:20). **He still speaks today, can you hear Him? I pray you do in Jesus' Name.**

> *When we call upon Him He will keep His promises to us.*

CHAPTER 3

The Voice of The Holy Spirit

"O Holy Spirit, descend plentifully into my heart. Enlighten the dark corners of this neglected dwelling and scatter there Thy cheerful beams." —Saint Augustine

Does the Holy Spirit speak to us? Can we hear the Holy Spirit when He speaks? The answer is yes! God speaks through His Spirit who is One with Him. He was with God before the foundation of the world. When you understand how powerful the Holy Spirit is in and to the life of the believer, you will seek to have Him remain permanently in your life. The Holy Spirit will empower you to heal the sick, restore the broken hearted, set free those held in bondage and preach good tidings to the down trodden. He will open your eyes to see great and mighty things that you wouldn't be able to explain or describe. You need the Holy Spirit to direct the course of your life.

> The Holy Spirit speaks the inspired Word of God to us; He brings the Word of God to our mind and heart.

The Holy Spirit makes God's Word come alive. He also enables us to hear and recognise God's Voice. Sometimes God's Word to you may not bring instant comfort to you because He wants to shake you out of your comfort zone, during these times, the Holy Spirit will strengthen you so that you can obey God's instructions. There are even times when the Holy Spirit will ruffle you up until you are ready to listen to and obey what God is saying to you.

You need the Holy Spirit in your life to activate God's prophetic gift in you. God can give you a personal prophecy for individuals or corporate prophecy for a congregation or body of believers. Sometimes God reveals a prophetic word to intercessors to stand in the gap for a particular person or body of believers. This gift can only be utilised properly when one is in close communion with the Holy Spirit.

In addition, the Holy Spirit speaks to us through our life's experiences. He never contradicts or opposes the living Word of God. He speaks in unison with God and Jesus Christ. The Holy Spirit is distinct from the Father and Son, He is unique, and He lives within us to perfect the Will of God. The Holy Spirit will enable you discern the hearts of people around you so that you can respond to them in a timely and wise fashion.

Why do you need to hear the Holy Spirit Speak to you?

You need to hear the Holy Spirit speak distinctively to you so that you can walk in the path God had destined for you to take. You need to hear the Holy Spirit speak to you for some of these reasons:

- **For Guidance and Clarity of Your life's Purpose:**

    The Holy Spirit will make God's purpose known to you. He will clarify God's purpose for your life to you so that you are better informed about your assignment, He will also lead you to fulfilling that purpose. He will direct your affairs and will save you from failing. When Peter and the disciples drew lots for the replacement of Judas Iscariot they sought God's guidance to reveal to them the hearts of Barsabbas and Mathias so that they could make the right choice. The Holy Spirit guided them in choosing Matthias who was then added to the eleven Apostles (Acts 1: 15-26). When the Apostles became burdened with the administrative work to the neglect of their spiritual calling, they sought the Holy Spirit's guidance in selecting seven men from amongst the elders to look after the division of the food. The Holy Spirit suggested Stephen and six others who were presented to the Apostles for prayer (Acts 6: 1-6).

The Holy Spirit also told the apostles to separate Barnabas and Saul for the work, which He had called them. It doesn't come any louder or clearer than this! Are you hearing the voice of the Holy Spirit? You must identify who is speaking to you so that you don't miss the day of your appointment. These men then went out and accomplished all that they were set apart for (Acts 13: 1-12). The Holy Spirit will choose the right job for you because He knows what is best for you. There is no error of judgment found in Him, as He is the Fountain of all Knowledge and Truth. The Holy Spirit is not influenced by the caprices of men, He is not biased, prejudiced or power crazy and neither can He be bribed or bought. He knows what plans God has for you and He will ensure that you achieve this with His help.

- **For Direction In life:**

Have you ever thought about going in one direction but you were led to go in another direction? You wonder "what" or "who" made you settle for the direction you chose. It is the Spirit of God within you directing you in the way that you should go! You must consult the Holy Spirit for the direction God wants you to take in life. The direction you take in life should be determined by God and not by your feelings, siblings or parents. We might make plans but let God confirm them. In Acts 16: 6-15 the Holy Spirit prevented Paul, Silas and their team from going into the province of Asia and Bithynia but allowed them to go into the province of Macedonia, in each situation they obeyed the direction given to them by the Holy Spirit resulting in their success and birth of a new church in Philippi.

The Holy Spirit will speak to you when you are on the crossroads and interjections of life and you don't know which way to turn in, **He will lead you in the right path where you won't go wrong.** He is the best direction giver for your life's journey. Your failure to seek His help will result in you becoming a drifter. There are times in your life when you ask yourself "Should I", "could I" and "would I"; at these times you need to hear the Holy Spirit's voice saying to you "Go this way". Romans 8: 14 states that all those who are led by the Holy Spirit are the children of God. He will give you the exact information you require, He will never lead you astray. As believers we must obey the voice and promptings of the Holy Spirit because doing so will result in our success and renewal of our strength in God, *Pastor Adebowale Adesina of Power House International Ministries (P.H.I.M.) says it this way:-*

"Simple solutions come from hearing God's voice; life will stop being a puzzle when we hear clearly what God is

Chapter 3: The Voice of The Holy Spirit

saying. Everybody is dancing to one beat or another, who's beat are we dancing to. Before you make a decisive decision that has the ability to alter the course of your life you need the Holy Spirit to tell you whether you are on the right path or not. The counsel of God is the assurance of His commitment to you in the midst of difficult situations about what direction you should take. The strategies and formulas for a victorious life come from God and not from man. The secret of divine success comes from God".

The Holy Spirit will guide your steps in life when you feel tired and weary. His role is to help you in every area of your life where you need His help. Sometimes He will guide you to those who will help you along the way. You must act on His instruction so that you don't lose the opportunity to make light the burdens you have been carrying. You might wonder why the Holy Spirit will want to send you to a particular person when they do not know you and have never set eyes on you before! Be assured that the Holy Spirit knows who is best to help you.

There was a time when my sister and I were going through challenging times in our lives. I heard God clearly asking me to call a particular person up to arrange a meeting with her to counsel us. When I told my sister about God's Word to me, she readily agreed with me as she had received God's leading to do the same. I went ahead and arranged the appointment. However, on my way to the meeting I began to hear varying voices in my head telling me that I was about to embarrass myself, therefore I should turn back and make my way home. I crossed the road to catch the bus to take me home but the bus never came. I therefore continued on my initial journey as God had instructed me to do, hesitantly making my way to the meeting. As I left the meeting that day, it dawned on me that God had gone ahead of me to prepare the heart of this person to be receptive to all that I had to say. I received clear direction for my life at that meeting.

The Holy Spirit will always lead you to do the right thing provided you make room for Him in your life.

- **For Speaking With Courage And Boldness:**

Simon Peter who was once a shy and fearful person became bold when the Holy Spirit overshadowed him. He spoke with authority before the rulers of the people, the Noble men and the Sanhedrin. He spoke without fear and intimidation as he defended his mission in life. When people saw him speak with eloquence they were astonished at his transformation. 2 Timothy 1: 7 states that God has not given us the Spirit of timidity, but of power, of love and of a sound mind. *We can see from Peter's life that the presence and power of the Holy Spirit in his life gave him:*

Boldness- He was able to stand up and witness for Christ in front of a large crowd

Soul winning ability- He led 3,000 people to Christ in one day

We need the Holy Spirit in our lives so that we can do what seems impossible to men. God has promised to bless us (believers) with His Spirit so that we will not walk in darkness but in the light. The Holy Spirit will cause you to have Godly confidence and boldness to do the things that you have not done before. You will not fear when you stand before your accusers because confidence in God will cause you to speak with authority. You will not be flabbergasted or become a stuttering stammerer when you stand before men of noble birth rather you will speak as an orator who is versed in his subject. He will take you to places that you can't go in your own strength. For example, when you are going for an interview that you think is beyond your remit, ask the Holy Spirit to go before you and to endow you with confidence and boldness to confound your examiners.

But when they deliver you up, do not be anxious about how or what you are to speak; for what you are to say will be given you in that very hour and moment, For it is not you who are speaking, but the Spirit of your Father speaking through you. Matthew 10: 19-20 (AMP).

- **For Discernment:**

The Holy Spirit will enable you identify God's voice from the other voices you hear around you daily. He will also give you a discerning heart to know when you are being deceived by others. For instance, when Ananias and Sapphira tried to deceive Simon Peter after they had sold off their land and kept a portion of the proceeds for themselves, the Holy Spirit showed Peter their deceit. If Peter had not been discerning, he would have been fooled by them (Acts 5: 1-10); just as Joshua was deceived by the Gibeonites into entering a pact to protect them, which the Israelites later regretted. Had Joshua sought the Lord's face before acting, God would have revealed the Gibeonites' deceit to him to safeguard Israel's interest. The Gibeonites later became a yoke to the children of Israelites (Joshua 9).

The Holy Spirit discerns the hearts, thoughts and intents of men. This is why we must seek Him before taking any life changing decision or committing ourselves to others whether socially or in business. 1 John 2:20 states that you have unction from the Holy Spirit therefore through Him, you will be able to have discernment. God will let you know the answers and solutions to things beyond your years both for the present and for the future resulting in your protection, acceleration and elevation.

The Holy Spirit will reveal to you the spirit operating within a person. The Holy Spirit once revealed to my sister that a particular person whom we knew had engaged in some form of activity that was not God glorifying. Without my sister going into detail, she mentioned her dream to this person's friend. To our astonishment, her friend said she knew whom my sister was talking about because this person had confided in her about the matter. My sister and I went home in wonder; we knew then that the Holy Spirit is truly the revealer of secrets and mysteries.

- **For Guidance Into All Truth:**

The Holy Spirit will tell you everything you need to know about a matter. He will reveal to you things others don't want you to know about. He will reveal the deceit of others to you to prevent you from being wounded. He will announce and declare to you the things that are to come. You cannot live your life without the presence of the Holy Spirit to guide you into living a righteous life before God. He can never speak against God or contradict

God's Word to you. There will be no room for the spirit of error and falsehood to take residence in your life, because the Spirit of Truth will flush it out (John 16: 13).

- **For Understanding The Scriptures:**

When an Ethiopian Eunuch had difficulty understanding the scriptures, the Holy Spirit sent Philip towards the chariot. Ordinarily without invitation Philip would not have dared approach the chariot but because the Holy Spirit led him, Philip obeyed and won a soul for God. The Eunuch was baptised with water and received the baptism of the Holy Spirit. **The Holy Spirit explains the Scriptures to you** in the manner that you can understand, that is why we have heard stories of illiterate people being able to read the Bible.

- **For Deliverance From Danger:**

Whilst Peter was in prison an Angel of the Lord appeared to him, awakened him from his sleep and told him to quickly follow Him out of the prison. Peter passed through the Iron Gate without disturbance and into freedom, what do you think would have happened to Peter if he did not see or hear the angel? (Acts 12: 3-11).

Whilst Paul was on a ship with his captors and their journey became hazardous, he heard God tell him that that there would be no loss of life. **Listening to the promptings of the Holy Spirit will save you from calamity and disaster.**

"Then ... Paul came forward into their midst and said, Men, you should have listened to me, and should not have put to

sea from Crete and brought on this disaster and harm and misery and loss. But [even] now I beg you to be in good spirits and take heart, for there will be no loss of life among you but only of the ship. For this [very] night there stood by my side an angel of the God to Whom I belong and Whom I serve and worship, and he said, Do not be frightened, Paul! It is necessary for you to stand before Caesar; and behold, God has given you all those who are sailing with you. So keep up your courage, men, for I have faith (complete confidence) in God that it will be exactly as it was told me" Acts 27: 21-25 (AMP).

- **For Spiritual/Church Growth:**

Jesus Christ recognised the importance of His disciples **having the Holy Spirit in their lives if they were to fulfil the great commission** He had given to them so He asked them to wait in the upper room for the outpouring of the Holy Spirit upon them. You need God's Spirit when you carry out this great commission to evangelise to the world. God will always prompt you through His Sprit to minister to particular persons at varying times; He alone knows the right season to lead you to them. Don't assume that your charisma will lead people to giving their lives to Jesus Christ, only the Holy Spirit can harvest a heart to listen to and receive the message of hope that you bring, your eloquence or ability alone cannot keep them permanently committed.

If the church is to take its rightful place in the land as God's voice to the nation it must seek God's voice. In the book of Revelation, God showed John the true state of the churches, although these churches were large and appeared outwardly progressive; God said that their activities and ways were not His ways. John wept because no one else saw or understood the vision; he understood that the churches needed to change if they were to control the spiritual climate of the land.

- **For Living A Victorious And Righteous Life:**

The Holy Spirit will cause you to walk righteously. He will cause you to be obedient and submissive to God. He will equally help you to take control of your flesh that seeks to dominate your spirit man. We all fall short at one time or another, we make mistakes that we regret later and sometimes we pay the price for our sin and suffer the consequences of it, however with the Holy Spirit's help we will be able to overcome our shortcomings. **He will weaken every evil impulse that has taken hold of your life that seeks to destroy you. He will liberate you from bondage** and from every veil of profound wretchedness that has been used to cover your glory. Every veil that lies upon your mind and heart will be destroyed by the power of the Holy Spirit for He will go to the fibre of your being to destroy all that was illegally placed there by others. He will restore and clean you up.

"In fact, their minds were grown hard and calloused [they had become dull and had lost the power of understanding]; that same veil still lies [on their hearts], not being lifted [to reveal] that in Christ it is made void and done away. Yes, down to this [very] day ... a veil lies upon their minds and hearts. But whenever a person turns [in repentance] to the Lord, the veil is stripped off and taken away. Now the Lord is the Spirit, and where the Spirit of the Lord is,

there is liberty emancipation from bondage, freedom). And all of us, as with unveiled face, [because we] continued to behold [in the Word of God] as in a mirror the glory of the Lord, are constantly being transfigured into His very own image in ever increasing splendour and from one degree of glory to another; [for this comes] from the Lord [Who is] the Spirit" 2 Corinthians 3:14-18 (AMP).

Jesus Christ said that His Holy Sprit will convict us of sin so that we can see the light and walk in the light. Without the help of the Holy Spirit we would not have the power to overcome weaknesses, habits and desires that cause us to walk off the path of righteousness (John 16:8-11).

- **For Counsel And Comfort:**

The Holy Spirit is our companion and comfort, He constantly brings comfort to our weary soul; His counsel is second to none. Jesus Christ said that the Holy Sprit whom He will send after Him will be our Counsellor, Comforter, Guide and Teacher. He promised that His Spirit will abide with us forever until His return (John 14:16). To be a true winner in life, you must start living each day with the Holy Spirit as your forerunner, pacesetter and counsellor, as the Bible states that by strength shall no man prevail.

Whilst my sister and I were planning to move to the United Kingdom from Nigeria in 1993, my sister had a dream during an afternoon siesta. Whilst asleep she dreamt that she found herself in the sea and was almost drowning- she can't swim. Out of nowhere came a "Hand" out of the skies to reach forth into the sea to grab hold of her, this "Hand" then drew her out of the sea to Him for comfort and safety. She pondered about the meaning of this dream and the revelation she received was that during her life's journey, she will be facing stormy and near death situations but God will be holding her close to Himself to protect her from sinking in the seas of tribulations causing her to come out victorious. We thanked God for the comforting message and assurance that He gave to her. We knew that He was assuring her that He will be her comfort throughout her sojourn in England.

For the Fruit and Gifts of His Spirit

Jesus Christ promised His Holy Spirit to us as a gift, He promised us that the Holy Spirit would be our comforter, counsellor, instructor, director and teacher. The Holy Spirit also helps us to develop the fruit of the Spirit, which are **love, joy, peace, long-suffering, goodness, faithfulness, gentleness and self-control**, which cannot be purchased or bought for a price. The Holy Spirit will transform you from within and this would be reflected in your relationships with others.

Galatians 5: 22- 25 (Amp), tells us about this fruit of the Spirit; *"But the fruit of the [Holy] Spirit [the work which His presence within accomplishes] is love, joy (gladness), peace, patience (an even temper, forbearance), kindness, goodness (benevolence), faithfulness, Gentleness (meekness, humility), self-control (self-restraint, continence). Against such things there is no law that can bring a charge]. And those who belong to Christ Jesus (the Messiah) have crucified the flesh (the godless human nature) with its passions and appetites and desires. If we live by the [Holy] Spirit, let us also walk by the Spirit. [If by the Holy Spirit we have our life in God, let us go forward walking in line, our conduct controlled by the Spirit.]*

I Corinthians 12 list the diverse gifts available to the believer, which will make him/her useful in God's Kingdom. The Holy Spirit gives each individual extraordinary gifts, abilities and strengths to help edify and build up the church. He gives us access to God and He intercedes on our behalf. If you feel that you are lacking in any of God's spiritual gifts ask Him to endow you with them now so that you can become an effective believer in the Body of Christ.

Your horizon will widen as you develop a **deeper understanding of Him.** The above will apply only if you have allowed Jesus Christ into your heart because He has told us that His Holy Spirit will in dwell us if we remain in Him. If you haven't given your life to Jesus Christ, now is time for you to do so, because Jesus Christ has guaranteed to deposit His Spirit within you to guide and lead you. However, this promise will only apply if you accept Jesus Christ into your life as your personal Lord and Saviour.

> *Salvation is God's gift to you, receive His gift wholeheartedly today.*

You can invite Jesus Christ into your life now by saying the following prayer:

"I acknowledge that Jesus Christ came to earth; that He died on the Cross of Calvary for me; that He resurrected and that there is power in His resurrection; that He ascended into Heaven to prepare a place for me... I believe that He has redeemed me from the penalty of sin and death. I confess all my sins to Him; I ask Him to forgive me now, to transform me and to start a new work in my life. I ask you Jesus Christ to come into my life so that I can live my life for

> *you. I thank you Lord Jesus for forgiving me all my sins and giving me eternal life. Amen.*

The Holy Spirit is calling out to you to come to Him without fear or shame and he is asking you to drink of the water of life without costs to yourself so that your soul will be refreshed and you will thirst no more. Whatever is preventing you from heeding God's voice is destroyed right now by the blood of Jesus Christ. Your desire to live a righteous life can only be done with the help of the Holy Spirit and not by your power. Jesus Christ is waiting to welcome you into the fold of believers, don't delay your decision.

> *"The [Holy] Spirit and the bride (the church, the true Christians) say, Come! And let him who is listening say, Come! And let everyone come who is thirsty [who is painfully conscious of his need of those things by which the soul is refreshed, supported, and strengthened]; and whoever [earnestly] desires to do it, let him come, take, appropriate, and drink the water of Life without cost" Revelation 22:17(Amp).*

Once you have given your life to Christ, you must begin to read the Bible daily and pray for the Holy Spirit's guidance and direction. You should ask Him to give you spiritual understanding and enlightenment. You may wish to start reading from the Gospel of John, which explains God's love for mankind and Jesus' willingness to sacrifice Himself so that man (including you) can be reconciled to God. You should also consider finding a local church that is Bible-based if you don't already attend one. You should introduce yourself to the pastor who will nurture you spiritually and build you up in the Lord; the same applies to those who once attended church but backslid for one reason or another. Return to the Lord and He will return to you.

In order for you to really say at the end of your life's journey that you have lived a satisfied, fulfilled and glorious life, the Holy Spirit must have been the controlling force of your journey. Without the infilling and support of the Holy Spirit you would only have existed but not lived. Don't underestimate the importance and power of the Holy Spirit in your life. He satisfies the thirst within us, He reassures us on a daily basis that we are loved by God.

CHAPTER 4

Praise, Worship & God

The worship most acceptable to God comes from a thankful and cheerful heart. —**Plutarch, c A.D. 100**

Do you know that your praise is music to God's ears, as He inhabits your praises? **God's voice can be heard in your praise and worship of Him**. God likes to soak up the praise emanating from your grateful heart. You must sing of the mercies of the Lord and make known His faithfulness to all generations (Psalm 89: 1-18). "Praise" is the expression of your approval or admiration for God whilst "Worship" is having reverential love, honour, respect and devotion for God.

Those who thank, praise and worship God know His true worth. You must thank God for His loving kindness which He has graciously bestowed upon you; you must enter His presence with thanksgiving and His courts with praise; dancing as you go along and rejoicing over the victories He has wrought on your behalf. Do you know that whilst you are

Praise God in advance of your coming blessings as your gratitude will cause Him to move on your behalf.

53

praising Him, He would work victory on your behalf? You must praise God for creating you and thinking you fit to be called His child. He created you to show forth His glory and to have dominion over the works of His hands (Psalms 8).

If you fail to open your mouth to praise God, He says He will raise stones to do so. Praise God in spite of the circumstances you might be facing because He is working things together for your good (Habakkuk 3: 17-19). When you praise God miracles happen and changes occur in your life. When you give God His due honour, respect and reverence, He will cause others to give you the same honour, respect and reverence in return.

> *"Let them give thanks to the LORD for his unfailing love and his wonderful deeds for men, for he satisfies the thirsty and fills the hungry with good things...He brought them out of darkness and the deepest gloom and broke away their chains. Let them give thanks to the LORD for his unfailing love and his wonderful deeds for men, for he breaks down gates of bronze and cuts through bars of iron." Psalm 107:8-16 (NIV).*

Lift up your voice with a voice of triumph, praise the Lord aloud with all of your might and be thankful in your heart to God for He is worthy to receive your praise at all times. If the heavens and the firmament can openly declare the glory of God day after day and night after night, why can't you do the same? If the Works of His hands can proclaim His love, why can't we do the same? (Psalm 19: 1- 4). The Angels in Heaven pay homage to God who is seated upon the Throne, and they continuously and ceaselessly give thanks before the Almighty Warrior — the Lion of Judah — why can't we humans do the same? God has saved you many times from death, calamity and disaster.

> *Do you realise that as you eat each time that God has saved you from chocking on your food and that you have a roof over your head that you can still call home!*

When Jehoshaphat praised the Lord in the face of adversity, it encouraged the children of Israel to be courageous to go into battle. He sent his choir to the battlefront to praise God who then sent an ambush against their enemy (2 Chronicles 20). Joshua did likewise when he went to capture Jericho, he sent the choir in front of the people of Israel to bring in God's Glory and he gained victory over Israel's enemies. **The joy of the Lord is your strength. When you feel weary, still praise Him and you will begin to see the impossible happen in your life.**

Your praise will cause others who have lost all hope to put their trust in the Lord. Praise changes the atmosphere of a situation; it brings the presence of God into a dreary situation. Lift your voice and thank God for the unseen battles He has won on your behalf. If you reflect deeply you will observe that there is always something to thank God for, you may not have all the things that you desire but when you look back, you will discover how far you have come. God has preserved your spouse, partner and family with good health and long life, don't take God for granted, thank Him for what He is doing in their lives and for what He has promised to do through them. God has surely delivered you out of the control and dominion of darkness into His Kingdom and marvellous light.

We must rejoice and praise God for avenging and vindicating us from the hands of our enemies. Lamentations 3: 21-27 states that the Lord is our loving kindness, our banner and His faithfulness are new every morning. God bestows upon us new mercies every day and His faithfulness never ceases. **He is our portion so we must be grateful to Him.**

When you praise God, He will come down from His Throne in His Shekinah Glory to manifest Himself to you. After King Solomon had praised, worshipped and magnified God for giving him the strength to build the temple, God appeared to him at Gibeon. God said that He would make His presence known

> *Your praise will make God take notice of you!*

and felt there forever provided the people continued the way in which they had started (I Kings 9: 1-3; II Chronicles 7:1-3).

King David said in I Chronicles 17:20-21 that there is none like our God nor is there any other God besides Him. God's glory is well known and famed throughout the ages; the wise will acknowledge Him for His goodness and faithfulness towards mankind for He has redeemed them as His chosen race. He also said in Psalm 71:21-23 that his lips will shout for joy when he praises the Lord and his tongue will talk of God's faithfulness and righteousness. Sing to the Lord a new song and worship before the Lord in the beauty of His Holiness. Make a joyful noise and melody unto God wherever you are. You don't always have to shout out, you can hum a praise song whilst carrying out your tasks at work, when walking down the street or when you are on your bed. Always have a reason to praise the Lord from your heart.

So why should you praise God?

You should praise Him because He is deserving of your praise, He is worthy to receive all your glory, honour and adoration. Praise Him when you face adversity, challenges and temptations because He will bring comfort to your heart and help you through the situations you are facing.

And when should you praise God?

You should praise God at all times, every day, every time, every hour, indoors and outdoors. You should offer sacrifices of praise to God both in good times and in bad times, in times of abundance and leanness, so that in times of difficulty your burdens will be lifted and His peace will reign. As you do so, His blessings and miracles will be poured out on you.

> *In all things praise His Name.*

And how should you praise Him?

You should praise God in any manner you want. You can praise God with your mouth (Psalms 71:8); with your hands (Psalms 134:2); whilst standing (Psalms 135:1-3); with your dancing (Psalms 150:4); with your music, with walking and leaping (Acts 3:8) and with your bowing and kneeling. God can certainly be heard in your praises, He speaks whilst you are still praising Him. He will bombard you with gifts when you glorify Him. **If you want to hear God speak, start praising Him in any manner, form or way that you are accustomed to and He will rise up to take notice of you.**

CHAPTER 5

The Voice Of Wisdom

"If any of you lacks wisdom, let him ask of God, who gives to all liberally and without reproach, and it will be given to him" —James 1:5 (NKJV).

To live a victorious life you need to hear the voice of wisdom. You need God's knowledge and understanding to achieve your life's purpose. Human intelligence is not sufficient for the long journey you have ahead of you as you will need something extra to make you stand out above the crowd and to bring you to the notice of great achievers. When you ask God for wisdom, He will show you great and mighty things not discernable by the human eye (Jeremiah 33:3).

Being brainy and crafty is one thing but having Godly wisdom coupled with discretion is another. Human wisdom can only take you so far before people begin to source you out. Godly wisdom cannot be manufactured, faked or hidden away; you can buy information but not wisdom. **William Shakespeare** said, "*Wisdom cries out in the streets, and no man regards it,* whilst **François, Duc De La Rochefoucauld** said "However glorious an *action in itself, it ought not to pass for great if it be not the effect of wisdom and intention".*

Having intellect without common sense is useless; it is like a ship without a sail or a rudder. Without common sense to lead and guide intellect, intellect is like a volcano waiting to explode. Intellect without wisdom is fatal for the believer- you cannot acquire common sense, it is gained by apprised experience. Moses received his schooling in Egypt where he learnt their wisdom and culture but coupled with that he exercised Godly wisdom in both his deeds and speech. This shows that an element of common sense is required above human intelligence- the Holy Spirit is the master of wisdom and common sense (Acts 7:22- 25). Hear what Apostle Paul said to the Corinthians concerning Godly wisdom in 1 Corinthians 2: 1-8 (NKJV):

> *Wisdom is prove of true discernment.*

> *"And I, brethren, when I came to you, did not come with excellence of speech or of wisdom declaring to you the testimony of God. For I determined not to know anything among you except Jesus Christ and Him crucified. I was with you in weakness, in fear, and in much trembling. And my speech and my preaching were not with persuasive words of human wisdom, but in demonstration of the Spirit and of power, that your faith should not be in the wisdom of men but in the power of God. However, we speak wisdom among those who are mature, yet not the wisdom of this age, nor of the rulers of this age, who are coming to nothing. But we speak the wisdom of God in a mystery, the hidden wisdom which God ordained before the ages for our glory, which none of the rulers of this age knew; for had they known, they would not have crucified the Lord of glory."*

Chapter 5: The Voice Of Wisdom

You need Godly wisdom, which brings with it a humble heart and spirit. King Solomon said that with all your understanding you should get Godly wisdom as this is what will qualify you to stand before great men. God is the greatest teacher of wisdom; the Scriptures are full of wise sayings that will help enlighten the believer in their walk of life. Some choose to reject the message of Jesus Christ because they are spiritually undiscerning. They are afraid of the Truth and what it would uncover in their lives. Jesus Christ came to bring revelation and illumination to the spiritually lacking and it is only when you receive His message that you will have real wisdom. God expects you to gain knowledge and understanding by sitting at the feet of those who are wiser than you are. He expects you to gain knowledge from your environment and the works of His creation. **He applied wisdom at creation so He expects us to apply wisdom in our daily lives.**

> *God's wisdom will make you stand out; it will distinguish you from the ordinary, common and mediocre.*

Ask God to open your heart to hear Him speak wisdom to you so that you can discern what is wrong and right to enable you live out your days in honour and dignity. Wisdom is God's absolute truth; knowledge is mans understanding of a matter. Divine knowledge is when God gets involved to provide a solution to issues that require dissection of the finer things! You know in part and see only a glimpse of the truth but when the Spirit of Truth opens your heart, then there will be revelation. Discern the times and you will be one step ahead; discern the heart of men and you will be ahead of them; discern how God wants you to do things and you will live wisely.

The discerning heart seeks God's wisdom and has a teachable spirit. A person who refuses to learn from others is curtailing his ability to gain social skills. You must have a desire and drive to learn and know more about God, people and your environment. You cannot afford to remain stagnant, never assume that you have reached the pinnacle of success that you stop learning.

Your ability to seek and hunger after wisdom will hold you in good stead. Wisdom will teach you self-control, perseverance and integrity that cannot be gained elsewhere except from the school of wisdom. Wisdom will qualify you to rule your home and nation. You need wisdom to speak against the evils in your society. You need understanding and discernment to know when to challenge people and when to keep quiet. The prophets of old knew when to speak up, when to pray and when to remain silent. They knew when to speak out against social injustice, spiritual depravity and moral apathy in their nation.

When God appeared to Solomon in Gibeon and asked him what he wanted, Solomon asked for wisdom, knowledge and understanding to rule Israel. Because God was pleased with Solomon for choosing wisdom above everything else God gave him unequalled wisdom except that found in Jesus. He also gave Solomon wealth, money and fame. Likewise God will give you what you have not asked for when you seek after Him and His ways diligently. Wisdom will give you the know-how to increase wealth.

If you were in Solomon's shoes what would you have asked God for? When you have the opportunity to converse with God, don't lose the opportunity by seeking the mundane; **rather ask Him for wisdom that will change your playing field forever!**

When Queen Sheba tested Solomon's wisdom by asking him difficult riddles she was astonished that he was able to answer all her questions on any subject she brought up, she was impressed with his level of wisdom as she had not found any other person as versed as he was in her journey of life.

Chapter 5: The Voice Of Wisdom

You must ask God for His knowledge, wisdom and understanding so that you can operate far above your peers, teachers and family in the affairs of life.

Scriptures where "Wisdom" spoke or was displayed are:

- Joshua 22:10-31: Phinehas, the son of Eleazar, the priest displayed Godly wisdom in averting war in Israel.
- Job 28: 28: The reverential and worshipful fear of the Lord is wisdom and to depart from evil is understanding.
- Psalm 32:8: God will instruct you and teach you in the way you should go; He will counsel you and watch over you all the days of your life.
- Psalm 37:30: The mouth of the righteous speaks wisdom and his tongue speaks with justice.
- Psalm 119:11: His Word have I laid up in my heart that I may not sin against Him.
- Psalm 119: 105: God's Word is a lamp to my feet and a light to my path.
- Psalm 119:99-100: I have better understanding and deeper insight than all my teachers, because God's testimonies are my meditation. I understand more than the aged because I keep, hear, receive and obey His precepts.
- Proverbs 2: 3-5: If you cry out for insight and raise your voice for understanding and seek for wisdom, you will surely understand reverence and the worshipful fear of the Lord.
- Proverbs 2: 6: It is the Lord who gives wisdom and from His mouth comes knowledge and understanding.

- Proverbs 7:4: When you say to skilful and godly wisdom that she is your sister and regard understanding as your intimate friend you would not fail.
- Proverb 8: Wisdom cries out, understanding raises her voice to you, good judgment calls for your attention, common sense and success are the right hand of wisdom, Godly counsel is found within her, nobility courts her attention and prudence is her friend. Wisdom is God's foundation for building a home and nation, run to them and you will be saved from disaster, destruction and doom.
- Ecclesiastes 10:12-14: The words of a wise man's mouth are gracious and will win him favour unlike the fool whose lips will consume him and bring him calamity.
- Ecclesiastes 12:11: The words of the wise are like prodding goads which are fired and fixed in place with nails unlike the fool whose mouth is like a dripping tap that never ceases.
- Isaiah 5:21: Woe is the one who is wise, prudent and shrewd in his own eyes
- Isaiah 50: 4-5: the Lord has given me the tongue of one who is disciplined and taught so that I speak a word in season to one who is weary. The Lord has opened my ear and I have not rebelled or turned back against Him.
- Luke 2: 40: Wisdom comes by growing and becoming more like Jesus Christ.
- 1 John 4:6: Wisdom says- *We are of God. He who knows God hears us; he who is not of God does not hear us. By this we know the spirit of truth and the spirit of error (NKJV).*
- Colossians 1:9 -10: states we should ask God to fill us with the knowledge of His will through all spiritual wisdom and understanding so that we can bear fruit in every good work that we do whilst growing in the knowledge of God.

Chapter 5: The Voice Of Wisdom

Wisdom knows what is right, true and real. **You cannot afford to be naïve, gullible or ignorant in understanding and wise counsel.** Seek God and He will fill you up with His wisdom. God said His people went into captivity because they lacked knowledge and understanding of who He is and what He is capable of (Isaiah 5:13). You can only have true freedom when you have the relevant knowledge to set you free.

> *God declared the following in Hosea 4: 6 (NKJV) "My people are destroyed for lack of knowledge. Because you have rejected knowledge, I also will reject you from being priest for Me; Because you have forgotten the law of your God, I also will forget your children"*

Joseph displayed Godly wisdom whilst he was in Egypt, which manifested itself before great men. The presence of God's wisdom on a person cannot be hidden for long; it would break out to shine before prominent men who are capable of promoting him/her. The wisdom of God resided upon Joseph that he prospered in whatever he did. In prison, he manifested the wisdom of God, which caused him to interpret the dreams of the butler and baker. The butler later spoke of him before Pharaoh who required his gifting to explain his dream, God revealed the dream to Joseph by the word of knowledge and understanding (Genesis 40 and 41).

When the men of Ephraim challenged Gideon for not calling them to fight in the war against Midian, his wise response to them prevented conflict and bad feelings brewing, *Judges 8: 1- 3 (Amp) states that "AND THE men of Ephraim said to Gideon, Why have you treated us like this, not calling us when you went to fight with Midian? And they quarrelled with him furiously. And he said to them, What have I done now in comparison with you? Is not the gleaning of the grapes of [your big tribe of] Ephraim better than the vintage of [my little clan of] Abiezer? God has given into your hands the princes of Midian, Oreb and Zeeb, and what was I able to do in comparison with you? Then their anger toward him was abated when he had said that."*

In 1 Samuel 25:1-42, Abigail displayed wisdom as she dealt with her foolish husband Nabal who had provoked David to anger by his uncouth and foolish words. By her wise words she calmed David's temper, thereby preventing David from killing Nabal and destroying her household. Her words appealed to David's reasoning and he withdrew his hands back from shedding blood on that day. David clearly remembered Abigail and he returned to marry her when her husband died.

When the King of Babylon conversed with Daniel and his three friends, he could not find anyone to match their ability and understanding as they exceeded others and excelled in all that they did. He found that Daniel and his friends were ten times better in all aspects of their lives than any of his advisors in his Kingdom. You need God's wisdom to have and maintain an excellent spirit. Daniel 5:12 states that Daniel had an excellent spirit and that he was filled with knowledge and understanding to interpret dreams, clarify riddles and to solve enigmas- knotty problems because the hand of God was upon him. Whenever Daniel had a problem he sought God's face for divine wisdom, understanding and the spirit of interpretation so that God will reveal to him the hidden secrets unknown to man.

In addition, Jesus Christ spoke in parables and uttered words that had been hidden since the foundations of the world. He spoke to the crowds in parables to explain the Kingdom of God to them. You need the spirit of wisdom and insight to discern hidden mysteries and secrets of the deep; **ask God to open your heart so that you can have an intimate knowledge of Him.** If you too want to be a shaker and mover in the Kingdom of God you will need divine revelation and insight from God. You need to accept that you have not arrived yet and that you are not the fountain of all knowledge.

You will only hear the Wisdom of God teaching, directing and instructing you when your heart is right before Him. God will become your teacher and He will show you hidden secrets. God will quicken your spirit to receive a greater understanding of Him and His ways.

> *"Let no one deceive himself. If anyone among you seems to be wise in this age, let him become a fool that he may become wise. For the wisdom of this world is foolishness with God. For it is written, "He catches the wise in their own craftiness"; and again, "The LORD knows the thoughts of the wise, that they are futile" 1 Corinthians 3: 18-20 (NKJV).*

Wisdom is flexible not rigid, it is adaptable not conforming, it is futuristic not archaic. Wisdom moves with the times and is not superficial. **Wisdom is spirit led and not self-serving; operating in wisdom will cause you to live a victorious life.**

CHAPTER 6

God Drowns Out the Enemy

> *"The floods have lifted up, O Lord, the floods have lifted up their voice; the floods lift up the roaring of their waves. The Lord on high is mightier and more glorious than the noise of many waters, yes, than the mighty breakers and waves of the sea."*
> —Psalm 93: 2- 4 (Amp)

Can you hear the thundering sound as God drowns out your enemy? God has promised us that every tongue that rises up against us in judgment we shall condemn Isaiah 54:17 (NKJV). Do you know that as a covenant child of Abraham God has promised to bless those who bless you and curse those who curse you - in their actions, deeds and thoughts, this is the heritage of the children of God. The Bible says that Christ by His death on the cross has redeemed us from the curse of the law; therefore no curse emanating from any source has the power to operate in your life. Do you know that God personally gets

> *The Lord will be your rock of escape and your fortress in times of trouble, He promises to deliver you out of all your troubles when you call upon Him.*

involved in your situation when your enemy causes you hardship or tries to prevent your progress? God says that the enemy you see this day you shall see them no more; you will rejoice before dusk sets in. He says that He will not keep silent until He has avenged those who ravaged you. God will flatten all those who gather together and strive against you. His hands are not shortened that He can't save you or His ears dull that He can't hear your cry for help.

To gain victory over your enemies you first need to hear from God. Hearing from God before going to battle is essential, without God disaster looms. When you are on the offensive you must first seek and enquire of the Lord about what strategy He wants you to apply in defeating your enemy. God will always give you the military strategy to fight the warfare. You must understand the rules of engagement before you go against the enemy. Satan plays rough so you must be prepared to get your hands dirty. Every time King David prepared for war he first sought God to ascertain whether God was behind him or not, he never went out against his enemies on his own accord. Judges 20: 18-48 tells us that the Israelites sought the counsel of God whether Israel should go to battle against their brethren (the Benjamites) or not and who should lead the procession. God said they should go, that Judah should lead the way and He would give them victory. Even when they first lost the battle against the Benjamites, they persisted because they knew God had assured them victory and they had consulted Him before embarking out on the attack.

> *"Surely the Lord God will do nothing without revealing His secret to His servants the prophets"* Amos 3:7 (Amp).

When you ask God to lead you into battle He will turn the mockery and taunts of your enemies on their heads and they will become a prey to their own schemes. He will expose their plans and strategies to you so that you are prepared when you face them. We know that God frustrated Harman's plans against Mordecai by allowing Mordecai to find favour in the king's eyes. God also caused Harman to be hanged on the gallows that he had prepared for Mordecai (Esther 4 -7).

God also showed Jeremiah the conspiracy his enemies frequently had against him; God frustrated their plans and their plans came to nothing. **When you are familiar with God's voice He will reveal the hearts and the intents of men around you.** He would reveal their schemes against you so that you can take precautionary steps to ward of their attacks. Jeremiah's enemies thought they could kill him but God frustrated their plans. Jeremiah called God the Mighty One in his life, when his enemies attacked him, they always stumbled and fell before him (Jeremiah 11: 18-23). What do you think would have happened if Jeremiah had not sought God in all that he did? He would certainly have been sent to oblivion!

> *"Plead my cause, O LORD, with those who strive with me; Fight against those who fight against me. Take hold of shield and buckler, And stand up for my help. Also draw out the spear, And stop those who pursue me. Say to my soul, "I am your salvation." Let those be put to shame and brought to dishonour Who seek after my life; Let those be turned back and brought to confusion Who plot my hurt. Let them be like chaff before the wind, And let the angel of the LORD chase them. Let their way be dark and slippery, And let the angel of the LORD pursue them. For without cause they have hidden their net for me in a pit, Which they have dug without cause for my life. Let destruction come upon him unexpectedly, and let his net that he has hidden catch himself; into that very destruction let him fall." Psalm 35: 1-8 (NKJV).*

Your enemy could be your laziness, adultery, or idolatry, which seeks to choke and master you, take these weaknesses to God in prayer so that He can give you the strength to overcome them. Don't allow satan to steal your blessing nor allow sin prevent you from inclining your ears towards God to hear what He has to say concerning your matter. Apostle Paul said that sin took a hold of his life to strangle God's peace out of him but God delivered him from the law of sin and death. Paul said that he didn't understand his own actions as he sometimes did what he didn't want to do. He sought to live a pure and holy life but he failed many times by doing the very things he despised (Romans 7: 4-25). He recognised that only God could free him from the clutches and snares of the power of sin and death (Romans 8). King David said in Psalm 4:1 that when he was hemmed into a corner, he cried to God who heard his cry and He had mercy upon him. Don't think that you are so strong that you cannot fall, don't take things for granted or deceive yourself; be alert to the tactics of the devil who would want to use your innate weaknesses to control you.

God will always sit up and come to your rescue. He will send His ministering angels to you to defend your cause. God may even use others to bring you out of your miry pit. In Psalm 124, David thanked God for giving Israel victory over their enemies. He said if God had not been on their side, their enemies would have quickly swallowed them up alive. God will not sit back and allow the enemy to tread over you. He will rise from His Judgment Seat and move His right Hand on your behalf. God will give our enemies to us as prey so that we can wring their necks and have complete victory over them. When Daniel called to God his prayer was hindered by satan for twenty-one days. Daniel kept praying to God until he saw the full manifestation of his prayers. An angel appeared to him to let him know that God had answered his prayers on the first day and that he had been sent to deliver the answers but satan had obstructed his path, however angel Michael, the archangel came to his aid in the Name of the Lord. This shows us that satan never relents in his efforts to tire the saints of God and that it takes only the Name of the Lord to defeat him. **You must remind satan that the Lord has rebuked him in your finances, health, family, work etc.**

You Have Been Empowered By God and Christ to Defeat the Enemy-

Prophet Zechariah says an angel showed him Joshua, the High Priest standing before the Lord and satan standing at Joshua's right hand to be his adversary and to accuse him before God. The Lord rebuked satan for opposing a servant of God before his master. He called Joshua a returned captive, a brand plucked out of the fire. You must never challenge satan in your own strength, but in the strength, power and might of the Lord who is mighty in battle for He has vanquished satan on your behalf (Zechariah 3: 1-3).

Again, when angel Michael and his angels fought against satan in Heaven, they overcame satan by the blood of the Lamb -which is the blood of Jesus Christ and by the words of their testimony; they didn't rebuke satan in their own names or power. The words of your mouth will either vindicate or condemn you at the time of trouble. Negative confessions will demoralise you before the battle begin, so don't be your own worst

> *God assures us that He has removed our iniquity and He has destroyed every contrary power, satanic control and stronghold that has held us down. He has broken us loose from everything that has refused to let us go hitherto, He has destroyed every limitation, restriction, manipulation, constriction and stagnation that satan placed on our life.*

enemy (Revelations 12: 7-11). Do not allow satan to bring fear into your heart. Angel Michael overcame him with the name of Jesus Christ. You too must go against satan with the name of Jesus Christ, do not go against him in any other name as the only name satan recognises is the name of Jesus Christ which is backed by power, might and authority. God has given you authority to openly rebuke satan in your life, start doing so right now in Jesus' name, cover yourself with the Blood of Jesus Christ every day before stepping out of your house. You cannot afford to allow satan to interfere with your children, family or business.

Every evil pronouncement, prophecy or oracle that has been spoken over your life by agents of darkness has been neutralised, destroyed and extinguished in the name of Jesus Christ. You have got to accept now that every opposition in your life has no choice but to bow to the name of Jesus Christ who has washed you with His blood. Don't allow ignorance and lack of knowledge of who you are in Christ hinder you from claiming your total victory.

God has given you the tongue and heart of a warrior so He expects you to open your mouth and prophesy against the things that stand in your way of success. God expects you to withstand the evil arrows shot against you by the might of His Hands. God has promised to shield you from the fiery darts of the enemy. He assures the believer that the Kingdom of hell will not prevail over them. He says that He has given us the keys of the Kingdom of Heaven so that whatever we bind on earth will be bound in Heaven and whatever we loose on earth will be loosened in Heaven (Matthew 16:19). Your goods are in the enemies' camp, your possessions are being sat upon by the recruits in the tent of the enemy, what are you going to do about it? The large grapes that you have desired to taste are in the hands of the giants; are you going to allow them taste the juice or are you going to take the bunch undamaged and quench your own thirst? Satan's agents have boasted long enough that you would not take possession of your inheritance, are you going to walk away in defeat?

God has placed an oracle in your mouth concerning your enemies so that they will not prevail over you. You will not be dismayed by their presence because God is your strong tower where you will run to for safety. We must guard and equip ourselves against these unseen enemies. Do not underestimate your opponent. **Paul tells us in Ephesians 6: 10-18 to be strong in the Lord and be empowered through our Union with Christ. He said we must draw strength from Him who has "Boundless Might". We must put on the whole armour of God to defeat all the strategies and the deceits of the devil for we do not wrestle against flesh and blood but against evil spirits and hosts of wickedness in high places. We must put on the complete armour of God to enable us to resist and stand our ground on the evil day and to stand firmly.** We must use the whole armour of God, which are the weapons of our warfare in order to succeed in our spiritual warfare. The above scripture says that:-

- **You must stand firm with the belt of truth buckled around your waist** - This means you must allow truth to reign in your life. You must remove falsehood and deceit from your life which will allow you to reprove the lies and deception of satan.

- **You must clothe yourself with the breast plate of righteousness** - This righteousness which is of Christ will set you free to live victoriously. We become righteous through our faith in Christ and not through any works of ours.

- **You must shod your feet with the preparation of the gospel of peace**- You can only have victory over satan's tactics when you live at peace with yourself, others and God. Lack of peace will birth strife in your life which in turn prevents you receiving your blessings.

- **You must take up the shield of faith which will allow you extinguish all the fiery darts of the devil** - By having faith in God's Word that no evil can overpower or befall you, you will live victoriously. Doubt will then become extinguished from your life and you will no longer live in fear because you will know that there is no power greater than God.

- **You must clothe yourself with the helmet of salvation to withstand the schemes of satan** - Do not allow satan to confuse your mind about who you are in Christ. God has assured you eternal life by your faith in Christ. There is always a war going on in the mind of the believer. Satan wages war against the believer's mind to confuse them. This battlefield of the mind can only be won when you know who you are in Christ and appropriate all that He did for you on the Cross of Calvary.

- **You must take up the Sword of the Sprit which is the Word of God** - The Sword of the Spirit is a weapon of spiritual warfare. You need the "Logos" and "Rhema" Word of God to minister to you on a daily basis. The "Logos" Word of God refers to the "Written" Word of God that inspires us as we meditate on the Scriptures whilst the "Rhema" Word of God is the "Spoken, Utterance" of God. The Word of God "Speaks" to you regarding your situation.

- **Having robbed yourself with this full armour of God, you are ready to pull down the strongholds of satan.** Every stronghold that satan has placed in your mind must be pulled down in the name of Jesus Christ. You must cast down imaginations and every high thing that has chosen to exalt itself against the knowledge of God in your life. Every negative thought in your mind must be brought into captivity to the obedience of Christ who reigns supreme over all things. We must be watchful and pray ceaselessly at all times in the Spirit.

As you begin to meditate on God's Word, it becomes alive to deal with any of the challenges that you might be facing. When I received the full revelation of the whole armour of God, I became free in my spirit, I knew from then onwards that I was not going to walk, live or sleep in fear as I had previously done because the power of God residing within me is greater than that which is in the world. As a child of God and co-heir with Christ, I have regained the power and dominion Adam lost in the Garden of Eden. I have the power to do great exploits. This is the heritage of those who belong to the Kingdom of Christ. I chose to no longer live in fear of what man can do to me, because I know that greater is He that is in me, than he that is in the world (1 John 4:4). God wants you to activate your faith in Him. You require a little faith like the mustard seed to live in the dominion which Christ has purchased you into. In case you don't know, you have already defeated and overcome satan by your union with Christ.

Now that you are in Christ, every veil of profound wretchedness, which satan used to cover your glory and to prevent your light from shining, has been destroyed from your life. He has clothed you with rich apparel and put a clean turban on your head. Jesus Christ has destroyed the yokes of oppression that held you down. He has freed you from the fowler's snare and the scorpion's sting. He has reaped to shreds the covering that made your life redundant, void and empty. He will not stand idle and allow satan to mess with your future and destiny. Every hindrance and delay in your life brought about by any veil of darkness has been removed. You must believe that Jesus has freed your spirit that had been locked up as a bird in a cage; He has released you to go forth like a stallion that cannot be bridled by anyone and victory shall be your portion (Psalm 35; Zechariah 3; 2 Corinthians 3: 14- 18).

Jesus Christ our Lord and Saviour defeated the dragon – lucifer — on our behalf and we must continue in that victory. The dragon thought that he could distract and destroy the Light, Seed and Savour of mankind from manifesting and accomplishing God's plans and purpose, but he was mistaken, his mistake caused him dearly. God will defeat your enemies as He did with satan when he was cut down from his high position in heaven. Those who have decreed in their heart that you would not succeed would be confounded by God and brought down to shoal (Isaiah 14: 12-19; *Revelations 12: 13-17).*

When you trust in God, He will give you peace in the place that you dwell and nothing shall make you afraid. You will lie down and sleep in safety, for your enemies will not have the audacity to come near your dwelling place. David said he called upon the Lord who saved him from his enemies. When men send words to mock, insult and ridicule you, take those words to God in prayer and He will reverse the potency of their words to your favour (Psalm 27: 1-6*).* Many may say that there is no help for you but God is surely the lifter and glory of your head. God will answer you out of His Holy Hill and will shame those who taunt, mock and reproach you (Psalm 3: 1-7). God says that when the enemy comes against you like a flood, the Spirit of the Lord will lift up a standard against him and put him to flight before you (Isaiah 59: 19). God will make you hear the sounds of defeat from your enemies' camp as every invention; scheme and conspiracy planned against you will be swept away by God's flood.

Chapter 6: God Drowns Out the Enemy

The Lord will be a fire around you and He will openly rebuke satan on your behalf.

You must recognise that the victory God wrought on your behalf is perpetual and eternal as such you must go and live a victorious life. You have been empowered to destroy everything that stops you from living the life of an achiever and a conqueror as God has already drowned out your enemy.

CHAPTER 7

God's Word Manifested in Season

"You will make your prayer to Him, He will hear you, And you will pay your vows. You will also declare a thing, and it will be established for you; So light will shine on your ways"
—Job 22: 27-28 (AMP).

The manifestation of God's Word comes in due season. At the appointed season God brings His Word to light (Titus 1: 3). God's answer comes at the right time and His timing is always perfect. God will return to you, according to His Word to fulfil all His promises He has made to you. No matter how it looks on the outside, know that God will not withhold any good thing from you. He will give you more abundantly than you dare to ask, dream or hope. All you have to do is remind God of His promises and watch His promises become manifest in your life (Ephesians 3: 20).

God's Word for Expectant Mothers/Fathers -

You shall not be barren. No matter the challenges that you are facing, God can be relied upon, He will hearken to your cry and come through for you. He will answer you from the Heavens and grant your petitions. If you are trusting God for the fruit of the womb for a child to call your own know for sure that He will look on your affliction and remember you just as He remembered Sarah. God appeared to Abram and promised him that Sarah, his wife would bear a son for him in his old age. Although they both doubted God's promise, He made them understand that He is the God who never fails, recants on His promises or Word. God promised Abram that his offspring would be like the stars- uncountable (Genesis 15: 1-5). In accordance with God's Word, Sarah later conceived and gave birth to Isaac at the appointed time. (Genesis 18:9-15).

God's miracle will not tarry a single day in your life. God will return to you according to the time of life to birth those blessings into your lap. You might be waiting upon the Lord for your own bundle of joy, and you are beginning to despair that God's promises to you is long overdue, just like Abram and Sarah, know that God will come through for you. All the years you have laboured will not be for nothing, God will provide your own child who will inherit all that you have stored up through the years, and another person would not take or occupy your child's place. *Isaiah 54: 2-4 (Amp) says you should, "Enlarge the place of your tent, and let the curtains of your habitations be stretched out; spare not; lengthen your cords and strengthen your stakes, For you will spread abroad to the right hand and to the left; and your offspring will possess the nations and make the desolate cities to be inhabited. Fear not, for you shall not be ashamed; neither be confounded and depressed, for you shall not be put to shame. For you shall forget the shame of your youth, and you shall not [seriously] remember the reproach of your widowhood any more."*

You may go down to the gates mourning but you will come back with joy in your heart. You will not remember the shame or reproach of your past. No matter how old you are, God is saying to you rejoice because more will be your children than the woman who has. You will not have to wait too long before your time draws near to deliver that miracle child. God's set time for your miracle to be birth has come. 1 Samuel 1: 10-17 states that when Hannah became distressed because of her inability to bear children she went to the House of the Lord and poured out her soul in agony to God. Although her actions were misjudged by Eli who could not decipher her words, Hannah's words were not lost on God who heard her cry and made her to conceive and bear a son whom she later she called Samuel. God remembered Hannah and gave her a child of destiny (Samuel) and He caused her to laugh so also will He cause you to laugh (1 Samuel 1 and 2:1-11). Hannah also went on to have more children.

God came through for Manoah's wife when she was barren, God sent an angel to tell her that in answer to her prayers He will give her a son (Samson) who would be a Nazirite to God. She later bore a son according to the prophecy given to her (Judges 13). God says that the pregnant amongst us will not miscarry and there will be no more barren in our midst, that every dried and arid place in our lives will become fertile and that we will bear much fruit. God has ordained children to be a blessing and He would keep His promise to you to give you that child you desire. He will fulfil the number of your days (Exodus 23: 26).

There was a rich and influential Shunammite woman who bestowed kindness on Elisha. Elisha took notice of her and enquired of her need so that he could bless her. Gehazi, his servant told him that she was barren. Elisha called her and prophesied to her that in due season she would bear a son. The woman could not believe it and asked Elisha not to lie to her. Without fail, the Shunammite woman became pregnant and bore a son (11 Kings 4: 8-17). Although the woman's son later became sick and died, Elisha restored the boy back to life because the word of God cannot fail.

> *"Behold, children are a heritage from the Lord, the fruit of the womb a reward. As arrows are in the hand of a warrior, so are the children of one's youth. Happy, blessed, and fortunate is the man whose quiver is filled with them! They will not be put to shame when they speak with their adversaries [in gatherings] at the [city's] gate" Psalms 127: 3-5 (Amp).*

God has ordained that your children will become your 'Heritage'; they will become like arrows in your hands. Your house will be filled with them and they will become notable, remarkable and distinguishable amongst men. The sacrifice you have put into making them achievers will not be wasted. You shall certainly reap the benefits of your parental nurturing. Psalms 144: 12 says your sons shall be as plants grown large in their youths and your daughters shall be as sculptured corner pillars hewn like those of a palace. Your children will be pillars in your community; they will not be troublemakers. **You must believe that the children God will give you and has already given you will be for signs and wonders and they will rise up to put your family's name on the world map, they shall take centre stage in the gathering of the people (*Isaiah 49: 1- 2*).**

Just as God swore to David that One of his Seed will sit upon His Throne, so also will your children rise up to sit higher than their peers. God has sworn to open your womb and bring forth a seed to carry your name to the next generation. Your children shall increase upwards and you will always have descendants to continue your lineage. Don't worry when the doctors tell you that you can't have that child; that you have gone through menopause; that your ovaries cannot produce eggs or that you or your spouse is infertile, hold on to God's word for the manifestation and fulfilment of your hope. God promises that your descendants shall be like the sand, your children would be like grains and their names will not be cut off before Him (Isaiah 48:19).

Do you sometimes wonder whether God's words are true? God says He watches over His words to make sure that every word spoken is fulfilled. Isaiah 65: 24 states that even before you call on the Lord He will answer you and whilst you are still speaking, He will hear you. Do not give up in your heart, but continue to hold on to God's promises. God said for everyone who keeps on hoping and asking will receive what they ask for. You must keep on seeking and you will find the answers you are looking for and if you keep on knocking, the door of favour will be opened for you.

A friend told me her testimony about how she waited upon the Lord for almost six years after her marriage to become pregnant. She said she had attended a particular prayer meeting in her church when the Pastor called out expectant mothers and fathers. She said that she and her husband came out for the prayer believing God for the blessing of the womb despite the doctors telling her that she was barren. She said whilst the Pastor was praying, he specifically said to all those who had come out in faith that it was their time to conceive, carry and bear a child according to God's Word. She held onto God's Word and saw the manifestation of her hope come to pass. She had postponed her IVF treatment due to financial challenges and was praying to God for a financial breakthrough when she became pregnant. When she told her Doctor the good news he was sceptical about her truly conceiving until he carried out an ultrasound scan to confirm her testimony. To God's Glory not only did she give birth to one child, without any intervention from the Doctor, she gave birth to another child a few years later. God's Word never fails to accomplish the purpose for which it was sent. Once He has spoken it, it must be fulfilled.

God's Word will not fail in your life. Here are some scriptures to remind you of God's promises, meditate on these scriptures daily:-

- **Psalm 92:12-15** — you shall still bear fruit in your old age and you shall be full of sap and vitality and your life shall be a living memorial.

- **Psalm 113:9** — He makes the barren woman to be a homemaker and joyful mother of (spiritual) children.

- **Job 42: 10-17** — And the Lord turned the captivity of Job and restored his fortunes, when he prayed for his friends; also the Lord gave Job twice as much as he had before… And the Lord blessed the latter days of Job more than his beginning… He had also seven sons and three daughters… After this, Job lived 140 years, and saw his sons and his sons' sons, even to four generations.

- **Isaiah 8: 18** — I and the children whom the Lord has given me are for signs and wonders that are to take place.

- **Isaiah 26:3** — You will keep him in perfect peace, whose mind is stayed on You, because he trusts in You.

- **Isaiah 41:10** — Do not be afraid for I am with you. Do not be dismayed for I am with you. I am your God and Strength. I will hold you and retain you.

It is also God's wish that you are emotionally, spiritually and mentally sound. He does not want you to be lacking in any area of your life. Some are emotionally barren because they endured an abusive childhood, some are spiritually barren because they failed to connect with God and have left the path of righteousness whilst others may be mentally barren because they have lost their sensibilities and have become stunted in their growth. If you fall into anyone of the above situations you must believe God's Word when He says that He wants you to prosper in every aspect of your life. God wants you to expect great things in your life. If you are feeling low and downtrodden, know that God will rejuvenate you and quicken you to become a fruitful and productive person.

God's Word for Singles-in-Waiting -

> "...But for Adam there was not found a helper comparable to him. And the LORD God caused a deep sleep to fall on Adam, and he slept; and He took one of his ribs, and closed up the flesh in its place. Then the rib, which the LORD God had taken from man, He made into a woman, and He brought her to the man. And Adam said: "This is now bone of my bones And flesh of my flesh; She shall be called Woman, Because she was taken out of Man." Therefore a man shall leave his father and mother and be joined to his wife, and they shall become one flesh. Genesis 2:20-24 (NKJV).

God is the creator of all things, when He saw that Man (Adam) whom He had created was alone, He caused Man to fall into a deep sleep and brought forth a woman from the rib of Man (Genesis 1). **Do not fret because you are still single rather meditate on what the scriptures say and decree your desired result into existence.** Proverbs 18: 22 states that when Godly men find a wife they find a good thing and favour from the Lord. Philippians 1: 6 states that God who has started a good work in your life will bring it to fruition. If it is your wish to marry or remarry don't become scared that what you are hoping for will not materialise. Wherever your future spouse is on this planet God will manoeuvre them around to link up with you.

Jesus Himself confirmed this in Matthew 19: 4-6, that **God created man and woman for each other, therefore God will provide your own partner for you.** You are therefore capable of growing into the fullness of marriage. When people say to you that they don't believe that you are the marrying type, let them know that God has given you all that you will need to make a marriage work.

After Ruth's husband (Mahlon) died, she expected to remain a widow but God had better plans for her. Boaz redeemed her as her husband's nearest kinsman and she lived peacefully afterwards. You may have been mocked and ridiculed, don't worry, God will come through for you when you least expect. Don't allow others to force you into marrying out of the will of God because they won't hang around when problems occur. The Lord has promised a home of rest for you, no matter how long it tarries; wait for God's prepared rest as you will find His peace there.

> *"Yes, the sparrow has found a house, and the swallow a nest for herself, where she may lay her young—even Your altars, O Lord of hosts, my King and my God." Psalm 84: 3 (Amp).*

If you are a single lady, do not be dejected or down trodden for the Lord your maker will open doors beyond your imagination and bring forth your own Boaz who will be your prince. You need not throw yourself at every available man to get his attention and a ring on your finger,

God's Word holds true and it will manifest itself at the appointed time.

because God is cooking up a blessing for you in due season; likewise if you are a single man, God would bring your own Ruth to you from wherever she may be and He would cause your paths to meet. If you desire to be married be assured that God has put that desire in you and He will perform it. You should put your hope, trust and faith in His Word (Romans 4: 16-24).

Know that God's Word will not fail in your life. Here are also some scriptures to remind you of God's promises, meditate on these scriptures daily:-

- **Genesis 1:28** — And God blessed them and said to them, Be fruitful, multiply, and fill the earth, and subdue it.

- **Job 42: 10-17** — And the Lord turned the captivity of Job and restored his fortunes, when he prayed for his friends; also the Lord gave Job twice as much as he had before... And the Lord blessed the latter days of Job more than his beginning... He had also seven sons and three daughters... After this, Job lived 140 years, and saw his sons and his sons' sons, even to four generations.

- **Matthew 7:7** — Ask, and it will be given to you; seek, and you will find; knock, and it will be opened to you.

- **Genesis 24: 12-27 (Amp)** — And he said, O Lord, God of my master Abraham, I pray You, cause me to meet with good success today, and show kindness to my master Abraham... And let it so be that the girl to whom I say, I pray you, let down your jar that I may drink, and she replies, Drink, and I will give your camels drink also—let her be the one whom You have selected and appointed and indicated for Your servant Isaac [to be a wife to him]; and by it I shall know that You have shown kindness and faithfulness to my master. Before he had finished speaking, behold, out came Rebekah, who was the daughter of Bethuel son of Milcah, who was the wife of Nahor the brother of Abraham, with her water jar on her shoulder. **And the girl was very beautiful and attractive, chaste and modest, and unmarried**. And she went down to the well, filled her water jar, and came up...The man bowed down his head and worshiped the Lord. And said, Blessed be the Lord, the God of my master Abraham, Who has not left my master bereft and destitute of His loving-kindness and steadfastness. As for me, going on the way [of obedience and faith] the Lord led me to the house of my master's kinsmen.

God's Word on Divine Healing -

Irrespective of what your doctor has told you about your health, the spirit of God would touch your body and heal you of all the diseases that have plagued you. It may be cancer, a tumour, or unexplained illness, God's Spirit will breathe new life into you. It may be that others are telling you about their medical ailment don't resign them to fate but rather let the words of your mouth bring hope to their situation as God will step in and cause them to be healed.

God says that signs and wonders will follow them who believe in Him. As a believer, your faith in God qualifies you to command for your healing with authority and boldness. Jesus Christ assures us that if we steadfastly believe in Him we will do greater things than He did. He said that whatever we ask in His Name, He will grant to us. You must not keep silent concerning matters relating to your wellbeing and health. God asks whether there is anything too hard, difficult or impossible for Him to do. The God of yesterday is also Lord over your life today; there is nothing too difficult for Him (Jeremiah 32: 26-27).

God showed Ezekiel dry bones that were in the valley and asked him to prophesy life back into them. Ezekiel opened his mouth to prophesy as the Spirit led him to do and he saw the impossible happen: breath and spirit entered the bones and they became alive. **The Word of God never fails.**

> *Again He said to me, "Prophesy to these bones, and say to them, 'O dry bones, hear the word of the LORD! Thus says the Lord GOD to these bones: Surely I will cause breath to enter into you, and you shall live. I will put sinews on you and bring flesh upon you, cover you with skin and put breath in you; and you shall live. Then you shall know that I am the LORD.'" Ezekiel 37: 4-6 (NKJV).*

When King Hezekiah became ill and was close to death, God sent Prophet Isaiah to tell him to put his house in order but King Hezekiah did not give up rather he cried to God for divine healing. God heard his prayers and sent Prophet Isaiah back to tell him that he would be restored to health and his life will be prolonged by fifteen more years (11 Kings 20). Similarly, when King David remained silent his bones wasted away so he called out to the Lord in prayer and God answered him. King David encourages us to call out to God who can be found and reached at all times (Psalm 32). 1 Peter 2: 24 says that **Jesus Christ personally bore yours sins in His Body and by His wounds you have already been healed from every disease, sickness or ailment that may befall you.** Hold on to God's words until you see the physical manifestation of your healing (Isaiah 53: 3-5).

God's Word on Financial Breakthrough -

> "'The silver is mine and the gold is mine,' declares the LORD Almighty. 'The glory of this present house will be greater than the glory of the former house,' says the LORD Almighty. 'And in this place I will grant peace,' declares the LORD Almighty." Haggai 2: 8-9 (NIV).

Your hard labour will not increase your wealth significantly. When you commit your finances to the Lord, He would multiply the seed in your hands. Anyone who boasts that he is a self-made person will learn that wealth comes and wealth goes but it is God who gives the power to sustain the wealth amassed.

As the bronze, silver and gold belong to God you must call them into your life from the four corners of the earth. You must pray that the wealth, which the ungodly has stored up for themselves, should manoeuvre and change course to locate you. The wise men located Jesus Christ and gave Him gifts when He was born, so also would the super-rich cut through thick forest to find you.

God declares in *Isaiah 48: 17-18* that *He is our financial redeemer who teaches us to profit and who leads us in the way that we should go, that if we had hearkened to His commandment then peace and prosperity would have been ours like a flowing river*. Our God is the chief accountant of our lives, when we get Him involved in our finances He will always keep our account in credit. When you trust Him to take care of your finances, you will have peace like a flowing river. You must not cease petitioning God for financial favour and blessings, He created us to be fruitful, productive, and resourceful. God will teach your hand to trade and to profit, He will make known to you the

> *It is God alone who can give you the power to create, retain and multiply wealth.*

market know-how, and He will give you answers to difficult questions so that the rich will pay you handsomely. **God will crown your year with good things and your path will lead to abundant blessings** – however, this will only happen when you walk in faith and obedience to God's instructions (Psalms 65: 11).

God's Word on Promotion and Favour -

God will give you a mouth like that of a sharp sword and He will make you like a polished arrow to go forth to manifest His glory. He will raise you up to be a blessing to your generation and He will make you a light to the Nations. Your day of promotion is in God's Hands, though it appears overdue, He will remember you out of Zion in due season (2 Peter 3: 8-9). God says that He alone knows the thoughts and plans He has for you, He says that He has good plans for your welfare and future. God has planned your future before you entered your mother's womb and He has decreed your end from the beginning.

> *"Therefore I have declared things to come to you from of old; before they came to pass I announced them to you,... You have heard [these things foretold], now you see this fulfilment. And will you not bear witness to it? I show you specified new things from this time forth, even hidden things [kept in reserve], which you have not known. They are created now [called into being by the prophetic word], and not long ago; and before today you have never heard of them, lest you should say, Behold, I knew them! "Isaiah 48: 5-7 (Amp)*

Joseph was promoted from prison to palace in a single day. The day of your elevation is in God's hands and no one can delay it by their actions, if they believe they can hinder your progress they are deluding themselves (Genesis 39-41).

When God wanted to promote Bezalel, son of Uri, He spoke to Moses about it. God also spoke to Moses about Aholiab, son of Ahisamach. You must wait for God to promote you because when He does it would be in the midst and presence of everyone (Exodus 31: 1- 6). Psalms 23:5-6 states that God has prepared a table for me in the presence of my enemies and He has anointed my head with oil and my cup runs over, surely His goodness and mercy will follow me all the days of my life in this land of the living. **I will not have to wait until I have departed from earth and gone to eternity before I am promoted. My promotion starts now.** By God's providence Aaron and his sons were anointed, ordained and sanctified into the priesthood. God promised Aaron that the priest's office will remain in his lineage perpetually if he and his descendants remained faithful to Him.

> When God wants to promote you He will speak of you in high places. He will speak of you before those who have the influence, power and resources to make your dream and vision come true.

When God sent Moses to die on Mount Abarim, He asked Moses to appoint Joshua as his successor to lead Israel. God chose to promote Joshua in the presence of the elders and people of Israel by asking Moses to impart the Spirit of God he had upon Him. Joshua's status changed from that of a follower to a leader in one day (Numbers 27: 15-23).

The Lord said to Moses in Deuteronomy 1:6-8 that they had dwelt too long on the mountain so it was time for them to rise up and take possession of their inheritance. God has already prepared your coming promotion, it is your duty to rise up and occupy your position. The Lord has promised to make you a thousand times as many as you are and bless you; you must however open your hands wide to receive all that has been gathered up for you (Deuteronomy 1:11).

When God wanted to promote Samuel He spoke to him in the midst of all the other voices that were distracting Eli and his sons. Although Samuel was faithful in his service to God, he had not tuned his spiritual ears to know, identify and recognise God's voice. It took Eli to open Samuel's heart to recognise God's voice (1 Samuel 3: 4-11). When God wanted to promote Saul, He spoke through Samuel. In 1 Samuel 9: 16-17, God said that He would send Samuel a man, a Benjamite to lead Israel as King. When Saul appeared the Lord told Samuel that Saul was the man of whom He had spoken about. Samuel took the anointing oil and anointed Saul in accordance with God's instructions. On the day of David's own promotion, God spoke through Samuel again to rise up and anoint David as His chosen King. David went in one day from being a shepherd over sheep to being the Shepherd of Israel (1 Samuel 16: 12-13).

Isaiah 49: 23 states that men shall see you and prostrate themselves before you; Kings shall see you and rise for you because the favour of the Lord is upon your life. God will elevate and promote you to the place He has ordained for you; Kings will be your foster fathers and guardians and queens your nursing mothers; they will bow their faces to the earth and lick the dust off your feet - this will be your own personal experience. It will not be a tale or fable; with God all things are possible. All you have to do is listen to what the Spirit is asking you to do. Psalm 71: 5- 8 states that God is our strength and hope, from our youth we have placed our trust in Him, we relied upon Him from our birth and because of that we would be a wonder and surprise to people. You must not miss the day of your promotion. **God has declared your future, listen attentively to His prophecy for your life so that you don't waste any time.**

God's Word of Restoration -

And I will restore or replace for you the years that the locust has eaten--the hopping locust, the stripping locust, and the crawling locust; My great army that I sent among you. And you shall eat in plenty and be satisfied and praise the name of the Lord, your God, Who has dealt wondrously with you. And My people shall never be put to shame. And you shall know, understand, and realize that I am in the midst of Israel and that I the Lord am your God and there is none else. My people shall never be put to shame Joel 2: 25-27 (Amp).

In Jeremiah 32:36-44 and 33 God promised to restore the fortunes of the children of Israel, He promised to bring them back from captivity and to be their God; He promised to bless the works of their hands and to bless them with gold and silver. You know what? God kept His promises by bringing them back to Israel after they had served their time in captivity.

Our God is a God of restoration. God's greatest act of restoration was when He allowed Jesus Christ to die on the cross for the sin of mankind so that Jesus could reconcile man back to Him. We see instances in the scriptures when God chose to forgive and redeem His people who had fallen from grace. God is still in the business today of restoring lives. God will restore to us all the lost years that we have wasted through our sin, transgression or ignorance. He is a God of second chance.

God increases the strength of the broken hearted and sets them up on a place of rest. When you call upon the Lord for strength, He will wrap His hands around you to support your feet from sliding. When you have sinned and have fallen short of God's glory, instead of hiding away yourself in shame or feeling dejected, cry out to God for mercy and He will uphold you by

His saving grace. You must rise from the depression and oppression holding you down into a new life of hope. Once you humble yourself before the Lord and call out to Him, He would be attentive to your cry for mercy and restore you to your rightful place.

King Manasseh ruled Jerusalem for a period; he later disobeyed God who caused the commanders of the army of Assyria to take him in hooks and fetters to Babylon. He later repented and humbled himself before God who heard him in his affliction and brought him back to Jerusalem. After his restoration, King Manasseh set himself to restoring God's temple, which he had covenanted to do whilst in captivity (II Chronicles 33: 1-20).

> *Cast your burdens on the Lord and He will sustain you. Our Everlasting Father does not grow faint or weary; He will increase your strength and cause you to fly high above every challenging situation. You will mount up like the eagle soaring to greater heights because you have trusted and relied upon the Lord (Isaiah 40: 28-31).*

On several occasions when Israel sinned against God, He sent them away from His presence into captivity; however He later took pity upon them and restored them to the land He had promised their forefathers. When they returned to their lands they rejoiced and praised God in tears for his mercy towards them when they did not deserve it. Whilst in Babylon, Daniel prayed to God to set Israel free from their captivity, he asked God to hasten the day of Israel's deliverance and petitioned God for their restoration as He had promised in His Word. God heeded Daniel's prayer by assuring him that Israel's restoration will come at the time stated by the Lord (Daniel 9: 17-27).

God will release you from the bondages of your past. He will release you from the captivity of your mind and restore you to become a whole person- a man or woman of substance. When you feel out of your depth, cry out to the Lord who will hear your voice and bring you out of the dungeon of life. Call on God day and night and He will answer you, and hear your prayer for relief and draw you to Himself to find rest and safety. I pray that God will also restore to you all your lost years, favour and opportunities in Jesus' name; our God is the Restorer of lives, fortune and destiny.

God's Word Concerning His Provision -

Abraham took Isaac to the top of Mount Moriah in faith, trusting that God knew what He was doing. Abraham did not tell Isaac that he was going to be sacrificed on the altar of God. After laying Isaac on the altar, the angel of the Lord called out to Abraham to refrain from taking his son's life. The angel provided a lamb as a substitute to be offered to God. God supplied Abraham's needs at the exact moment he required it *(Genesis 22: 7-14)*.

> Our God will provide all our needs according to His riches in Christ Jesus.

Abraham had caught the revelation that God was his provider, so he called the place Jehovah Jireh meaning, "The Lord will provide". The Lord called again to Abraham from heaven a second time and swore to bless him and his descendants forever because Abraham trusted Him as his provider. God speaks in the stillness and when the wind is bellowing, can you hear Him? He speaks through dreams, visions and prophesies; make sure you are tuned in to God's frequency so that you can hear Him without interruptions.

God became Israel's provider when they left Egypt, they cried for food to Moses when they became hungry in the wilderness and he petitioned to God on their behalf. God heard their voice and provided manna for the Israelites to eat for forty years in the wilderness until they entered the land of Canaan (Exodus 16). They also became thirsty in the wilderness so they cried for water to quench their thirst, God heard their voice and He told Moses to strike the rock at Mount Horeb for water and Moses did so.

When you serve God diligently He will bless the works of your hands and He will make His provisions available to you, He will open the floodgates of Heaven to you. God said that if you obey His voice and His statutes and commandments that He gave to you then He will give you rain in due season and that whatever you sow you shall reap. Your sweat and labour will not be in vain. God will open to you His good treasury and you shall never be found wanting (Leviticus 26: 3-5). God says that your storehouses will not go empty, as He will replenish them with the provisions you need. He will set you high above your enemies so that they will know that you are blessed of the Lord.

God will give you a turnaround miracle as He did with the Israelites in the time of Elisha when King Ben-Hadad of Syria besieged Samaria (11 Kings 7). You must ask God to open His eyes to your written petitions.

Jesus Christ on a couple of occasions spoke to "bread and fish" and asked them to multiply to meet the needs of the multitude congregation and these tangible things listened to Him. Jesus made provisions for His people when they thought it impossible. God will meet you at your point of need, no matter how difficult things may appear to be, God made the heavens and the earth by the power of His great arm, therefore there is nothing too hard or difficult for Him to do. In Jeremiah 32: 25-27, God provided Jeremiah with the means to purchase a field and reminded him that there was **nothing too hard for Him to perform**. That is the assurance we have in God, that when we call upon Him earnestly He will answer us and show us great and mighty things, God will turn that emptiness around to fruitfulness.

God's Word of Peace -

God says He will give you peace in times of trouble. When you feel overwhelmed come to 'The Rock of Ages' and He would give you His peace in the midst of your trials. God says that the peace He gives us is different from that which the world gives.

In John 14:27, Jesus said that He has already bequeathed His peace to you not as the world gives to you. His peace is different from the peace given by the world as worldly peace is temporal whilst God's peace is permanent and eternal. God states that you should not allow your heart to be troubled, that you should not be afraid, neither should you allow yourself to be agitated, disturbed, fearful, intimidated or unsettled as He will be your peace, His peace is abiding and never ceases.

No matter what you trust God for He will supply all your needs in His own time. He is a God who answers in due season. His answers are never late; they are always at the right second, minute, hour, day, month, year or decade.

> *He assures us that when we call upon His Name He would answer us and be there for us. God has pledged and bequeathed His peace to you, rise up and find comfort in His words.*

CHAPTER 8

Obstacles & Consequences of Failing to Hear God's Voice

Frieda Stewart said "Sometimes the weight of the world will heavy my heart But I must remember to look to the one—who from the start.... Knew me before I took my first breath Loves me even though my heart is being torn from my chest. I must remember, although actions may play a big part in my fate, God loves me and watches me; sometimes all he can do is wait. Wait while I try to control all around, As I continue to ride on this merry-go-round. Instead of listening to God's divine holy voice, I choose to ignore, I have made this my choice. The choice to live life my very own way; with pleasure and hurt, competing each day. When will I lay down my very own will? Listen attentively, be quiet, be still. I know that for my life he has a plan. Will I trust him forever and rest peacefully in his hand? This is a choice that I alone must make. No one else can decide, it is my destiny, my fate ..."

Now that you have pondered on the above quotation, what do you think some of these obstacles are?

Obstacles to hearing God's voice

There are many obstacles to hearing God's voice, these obstacles stem from distrust itself, life's distractions, prayerlessness, pride or indifference. We should be cautious not to allow our past experiences with people and unrealistic expectations of God debar us from hearing God when He speaks to us in the present.

- **Distrust**

    When you lose confidence in God you distrust Him, this is part of human make up. When you stop trusting God, it follows that you will no longer incline your ears to listen to what He has to say to you. You may have gone through challenging times and felt that God was not there for you when you needed Him the most. As such you resolved in your heart not to trust Him anymore in what He says to you. We tend to shut out those we feel we have lost all confidence in, in order not to get hurt by them again. We unilaterally make a vote of <u>no confidence</u> not realising that we injure ourselves the most.

- **Life's distractions**

    When you become too busy with the affairs of life you no longer have the time and patience to wait upon the Lord for His next instructions. When your life is inundated with conflicting priorities you may feel that your work, family or finances comes first, so you put up a barrier in your mind to hearing God's voice.

Chapter 8: Obstacles & Consequences of Failing to Hear God's Voice

Abraham departed from his father's house and took with him some of his relatives (including Lot) without first seeking God's approval; they later became a burden to him. You may need to jettison the excess baggage in your life if you want to hear from God. For some of you it may be your friends, a habit, or a negative trait that is preventing you from hearing what God is saying to you. You must commit your life, finances and time to God. Ask the Holy Spirit to enlighten you so that you can jettison dead issues. It was only after Lot and his followers departed from Abraham that he heard God speak again (Genesis 13: 14-18).

Too much activity will steal your focus as life's worries have a way of stealing your attention and ear away from God. Always remember to take time out to rest from your busy schedule so that you can hear God. Learn to hear God's voice even when carrying out your daily tasks as He is interested in your daily affairs. Gadgets today vie for our attention as they draw our eyes away from God. In Luke 10: 38- 42 we read about Mary and Martha, Jesus told Martha that she was distracted with too much serving instead of focussing on Him. Don't allow too much partying, socializing and hosting of guests steal away the time you should be communing with God. Martha wrongly believed that her performance equalled acceptance with Christ. She forgot that it is grace and not works that will secure her acceptance in Christ. The same applies to you today; it is your obedience to Christ that will secure your acceptance in Christ and not your works.

On some occasions I had allowed life's worries to draw my attention away from God. I had discovered that whenever I wanted to have a quiet time with God I found my mind being flooded with a thousand and one things that I had forgotten to do or should be doing. I soon discerned that it is the wiles of the devil to draw my focus away from God. As a way of avoiding unnecessary distractions, I have learnt to keep a piece of paper beside me to scribble down the things that come to my mind which I have forgotten to do so that I can do them later.

Sin

Sin causes a separation from God. Sin keeps God out of our lives as it shuts us up and makes us recoil from His presence. Some may believe that their lives are filled with so much sin that God has abandoned them. They feel that God has stopped speaking to them so they give up seeking after Him. Some may be living in bitterness, hatred and un-forgiveness and have refused to let go of their past hurts. You must let go of everything that is holding you to your past so that you can hear God clearly. When we have un-confessed sin in our lives, we feel condemned. Romans 8:1 states, that there is now no condemnation to them who are in Christ Jesus. Confess your sins, transgressions and iniquities to God and **let Him free you to live in the freedom that Christ has purchased you into.**

Doubt and Unbelief

Some people are just sceptical about everything, they don't believe that God can speak to them; He might speak to other people but definitely not them! They refuse to open up their hearts to receive what He is saying to them. Some are like "Doubting Thomas" in the Bible who doubted that Jesus was alive; he had to see things for himself before he could believe anything being told to him, his motto was seeing is believing! However I must qualify his doubting heart here, because it can be said for him that he wanted to see and hear Jesus for himself and not believe what others were saying so that they don't mislead him. ***E.Y. Harburg*** *is attributed to have said, "No matter how much I prove and prod, I cannot quite believe in God; But oh, I hope to God that He unswervingly believes in me".*

Sometimes we not only doubt what God has told us about our future, we also allow unbelief to steal away our faith in God. It is so easy to believe the lies of satan who is continually whispering lies into our ears rather than God who does not force His Will upon us. Unbelief is the seed planted by satan in our heart and mind to cause us to disobey God, resulting in us losing our blessings. Don't allow unbelief to rob you of God's blessings. You have to prayerfully and consciously re-channel your mind to believe what God is saying to you. The Bible records that God punished the children of Israel on many occasions because of their unbelief which He equated as sin and disobedience of Him. We must be alert to satan's tactics who would want us to sin against God by continuing in unbelief. You must recondition and refocus your mind and ask the Holy Spirit to strengthen and enable you eradicate doubt and unbelief from your life.

Prayerlessness

When you fail to spend quality time in prayer, you fail to hear God's voice when He speaks. Prayer must not be a one-way communication stream, where you do all the talking, whining and complaining whilst God does all the listening. You must learn to remain silent in the presence of

God to hear what He is saying next to you. He is never tired of hearing from you like some people are inclined to do.

"Prayer does not change God, but it changes him who prays." - **Soren Kierkegaard**

"God speaks in the silence of the heart. Listening is the beginning of prayer."- **Mother Teresa**

So what do we say prayer is? G. Campbell Morgan states that, "Prayer is listening for God, hearing what God has to say, consenting to what God does say, asking of God power to obey. To neglect these things is to be powerless when we meet the lepers and the palsied men of the world."

Pride

Some refuse to hear God's voice because they believe He doesn't know what's best for them, they have allowed pride to becloud their judgement. Some, in their arrogance believe that they are better at controlling and determining their own destiny and therefore do not see the importance of God meddling in their lives. When God tells them to go right, they prefer to go left, so they ignore His voice by blanking Him out and ignoring Him completely. You've heard it said before that pride comes before a fall. The prophets of old warned the Israelites to stop being proud and haughty, however on many occasions the Israelites ignored God's voice because His warnings and discipline were not to their liking, they however paid the price for their foolishness.

The Fear of Man

The "fear of man" can hinder some from hearing God's clear instructions to them. Some have rejected God's

Chapter 8: Obstacles & Consequences of Failing to Hear God's Voice

Counsel to them because they have allowed the "fear of man" control them. There is no point in asking God for a "word" when we have no intention of obeying Him. The "fear of man" brings a snare but those who trust in the Lord will be saved. Some fear "men" more than they fear God, they forget that God is all powerful and that if they put their trust in Him, He will keep their mind in perfect peace. On my part, I too have fallen foul of allowing people to control me in the past which led me to disobeying God's counsel to my own detriment.

The fear of God is the beginning of wisdom. God will give you the required knowledge to deal with those who seek to control your life and affairs. Two notable examples of people in the Bible who allowed the "fear of man" to control them were:

1) King Zedekiah who rejected Jeremiah's prophecy that he should surrender to the King of Babylon because he feared the Jews (Jeremiah 8:14-24) and

2) Johanan son of Kareah and all the army officers in his company who rejected God's counsel to them because they feared the King of Babylon (Jeremiah 42).

Both men allowed the "fear of man" to control them and their decisions. Later what these men feared came upon them because they did not put their trust in God. Ask God to set you free from the fear of man.

- **Indifference**

Some are simply indifferent about God and what He has to say to them. They see all the evil in the world and feel that if God truly exists then the world should not be as bad as it is. They are sceptical about the things of the Spirit and believe that they can succeed on their own.

- **Lust of the flesh, lust of the eyes and pride of life**

    Lusting is desiring something that doesn't belong to you; and this desire consumes your thoughts and your life. Any one of these things tends to make us lose focus and our sense of hearing. We sometimes ignore God's instructions to us because we want to satisfy our own earthly cravings (1 John 2:15-16).

Having considered some of the obstacles to hearing God's voice now let us consider some of the consequences of failing to hear His voice?

Consequences of Failing to Hear God's Voice

There have been many occasions in my life when I disregarded God's instructions, choosing to "go my own way" and "doing my own thing". I must admit to you that the results were disastrous. The effect of not listening to God is often times more serious than the act of the disobedience itself. It is much better to heed God's voice and advice than to suffer the consequences of failing to do so. My prayer is that you will not feel condemned by your mistakes but rather you will let your mistakes act as an impetus to developing a better relationship with Him so that you can hear Him clearly when He speaks.

> *Then He said, "Go out, and stand on the mountain before the LORD." And behold, the LORD passed by, and a great and strong wind tore into the mountains and broke the rocks in pieces before the LORD, but the LORD was not in the wind; and after the wind an earthquake, but the LORD was not in the earthquake; and after the earthquake a fire, but the LORD was not in the fire; and after the fire a still small voice.*

So it was, when Elijah heard it, that he wrapped his face in his mantle and went out and stood in the entrance of the cave. Suddenly a voice came to him, and said, "What are you doing here, Elijah?" 1 Kings 19: 11-13(NKJV).

- **Purpose and Destinies of people are aborted or destroyed**

You have to identify the origin of every voice that you hear and ask the Holy Spirit to help you discern each voice. Purpose and destinies of people can be aborted or destroyed when God's voice cannot be distinguished from other voices. Don't allow people to cause you to sin by listening to them, God will hold you responsible for your disobedience. The fact that God remains silent sometimes does not mean you have to converse with the devil. You must know who to speak to when you feel down and depressed so that you don't become polluted by negative thoughts of the ungodly.

Genesis 3 states that when the serpent approached Eve to deceive her, he twisted God's words causing her and Adam to fall from grace. Eve did not discern that the serpent was lying to her; he succeeded in reasoning her out of God's will for her life. She ate the forbidden fruit and then persuaded Adam to eat some of it thereby buying into satan's ideas. The serpent persuaded Eve into believing that she was entitled to her own views, choices and desires. She in turn persuaded her husband to accept the ideology that God did not really like them enough to give them everything they wanted. As a result of their disobedience, God threw them out of the Garden of Eden and He cursed them.

We also understand that when the earth became full of people who spoke one language, these people settled in the land of Shinar and began to reason and talk alike. They began to listen to one another and decided to go their own way, and departed from the way of the Lord. The people of Babel were highly skilled; they were architects and engineers who were able to design novel things. They decided to build a name for themselves by constructing a tower that would reach to the skies. God decided to punish them for their arrogance and idolatry by bringing confusion into their midst, and changing their language. The voices of the highly intelligent amongst them swayed the masses to collectively destroy their future. God had a purpose and vision for them but they stopped listening to His voice and what He had to say to them (Genesis 11: 1-8).

> *A sure way of aborting your purpose is by refusing to heed God's voice when He speaks to you.*

Terah heeded God's voice to change his location so he took his family from Ur of the Chaldeans to go to Canaan but on his way he listened to the many voices around him and settled in Haran and died there, thereby aborting his destiny (Genesis 11:31-32). Abraham on the other hand hearkened to God's voice and left Haran to the land God had promised to show him. When Abraham passed through the locality of Shechem in the land of Canaan, God appeared to him again and promised to give him and his posterity the Land of Canaan provided he continued to obey, listen to and seek after Him. Abraham built an altar there to the Lord in thanksgiving (Genesis 12:1-7). Despite some hiccups along Abraham's way,

Chapter 8: Obstacles & Consequences of Failing to Hear God's Voice

which resulted in near calamities, He always went back to God for help. **Abraham's trust and faithfulness was accounted to him by God as righteousness (Romans 4: 1-3).**

Some abort their destiny because they choose to ignore God's instructions to them rather than lose face in front of their subjects, peers or family. Saul was anointed by Samuel as the first appointed king of Israel when the Israelites were displeased about judges ruling over them. His first assignment was to fight against Nahash the Ammonite whom he conquered as God gave him victory. Samuel later told Saul to meet him at Gilgal to renew Saul's kingship as the people's choice, however while waiting for Samuel for seven days the Philistines assembled to fight against the Israelites. In fear Saul decided to offer both burnt and peace offerings in disobedience to God as he did not like to lose face in front of his subjects. Just as he completed the sacrifices Samuel appeared. Saul found an excuse for his disobedience when challenged by Samuel, but God saw through them. Samuel told him that his reign would not continue and that God had appointed another person in his place. Saul wanted to feel important in the sight of his subjects but instead of his elevation he was demoted.

On another occasion, Samuel told Saul that he was to go out and defeat the Amalekites for what they did to the Israelites when they came out of Egypt. Saul was told to destroy everything that the Amalekites owned including the people and their animals. Although he killed the people, he spared Agag, king of the Amelikites and the best of the animals. God told Samuel that he had repented the day Saul was made king. Samuel rebuked Saul but again he tried to make excuses for his disobedience by apportioning the blame on his subjects. God told Samuel that he had regretted making Saul king. Samuel shook his hands off Saul and never saw Saul until his death. Saul had with his own hands ripped the kingdom away from himself and aborted his destiny; he did not need any enemy to do that for him (1 Samuel 15).

There was a young man of God who appeared out of Judah at Bethel to prophesy to Jeroboam as he stood by the altar to burn incense. God sent the young prophet on assignment and was strictly told not to eat anything or return by the way he had come. After completing his assignment the young prophet met an old prophet who lied to him. The old prophet gave him a false prophecy resulting in him disobeying God. God now sent the old prophet to tell him that he would die a painful death for his disobedience (1 Kings 13: 16-22).

Loss of God's Grace, Glory and Presence

When we refuse to heed God's voice we fall from His Grace and Glory. In the book of Ezekiel, God asked Ezekiel to warn Israel about mending their ways otherwise He would depart from amongst them. They failed to heed God's Words or that of His prophet, so God took His presence and His glory from the temple and from their lives. We must never get to the stage where God's Glory departs from our home, family, church or nation. Zechariah warned his people to heed God's warnings but they refused to listen or change their ways, so God became angry and stopped listening to them when they cried out to Him for mercy.

Chapter 8: Obstacles & Consequences of Failing to Hear God's Voice

We need God's Glory and covering on our lives if we are to go the distance. Don't allow pride to derail you as those who have tried going without God have fallen flat on their faces in shame and defeat.

- **Loss of Focus and Direction**

When you listen to what God is saying to you, you will not take your focus off Him. King Joash of Jerusalem became a king at seven years of age when he replaced Athaliah his grandmother. He kept his focus during the days of Jehoiada, the priest who was his uncle, but once Jehoiada died, King Joash aligned himself to the Princes of Judah and he forsook his God, choosing to worship idols instead. He stopped listening to what God had to say to him. When Zechariah, the priest rebuked him for his loss of focus, King Joash commanded that he be killed in the court of the Lord's House. King Joash, in turn, was killed by his own servants on his bed whilst sick (II Chronicles 24).

Another King who stopped hearing what God had to say to him was King Uzziah. He was sixteen years old when he began his reign in Jerusalem under the guidance of Zechariah who instructed him in the Way of the Lord. He carried out building projects; built an array of army which he strengthened and equipped and defeated his enemies.

> *When you fail to hear God, you lose your focus and direction.*

However, like many kings before him he lost his focus when he became strong, he became proud and refused to listen to Azariah, the priest's counsel who rebuked him for entering the Temple to burn incense on the Altar.

King Uzziah became enraged that he was corrected; he became cursed and died a leper (II Chronicles 26:16-23).

Unlike the two kings before him, Nehemiah rallied the returned exiles to rebuild the wall of the Temple and reminded them of the promises of God. When Sanballat and his antagonists constantly reviled the Israelites Nehemiah instructed his people to remain quiet and keep focused on building the temple, he told them to bring to their remembrance God's Word of deliverance to His people. By maintaining their focus on God, Israel completed the task on time (Nehemiah 4-6).

When Jesus Christ was being reviled and put to shame by His accusers who brought Him before Pilate, He remained silent. He did not want to be distracted by the voices, which sought to hamper and distract Him from His ultimate goal of dying for mankind on the cross so He maintained His silence and focussed on God's next instructions. **When it was time for Jesus Christ to speak out He did** because His mission had been accomplished and He had stood the test of His trials. When Jesus gave up His Ghost, the curtain of the Holy of Holies was torn in two from top to bottom. When God gives you an assignment or project to accomplish, it is wise to keep quiet until the accomplishment of that assignment (Mark 15: 1-5; 37-39).

Loss of God's Peace

When you fail to hear God's voice His peace departs from you resulting in you going through trials and temptations you did not foresee. Listen to what God has to say concerning your situation as He promises to strengthen your hands to withstand the tempest that may blow your way. God has promised to give you His peace like a river.

"Thus says the LORD, your Redeemer, The Holy One of Israel: "I am the LORD your God, Who teaches you to profit, Who leads you by the way you should go. Oh, that you had heeded My commandments! Then your peace would have been like a river, And your righteousness like the waves of the sea Isaiah 48:17-18 (NKJV).

Leads to Unbelief

After the Israelites left Egypt, they complained regularly to Moses who sought God's face. Moses constantly encouraged them to have faith in the God who delivered them from bondage. Moses told them that God was able to do all that He had promised their fathers. When Moses sent out twelve spies to the land of Canaan, ten came back with an adverse report causing the people of Israel to revolt again God resulting in disastrous consequences for Israel. Although God had promised Israel victory over Canaan and that wherever their feet tread upon He would give to them, they lost their blessings through their unbelief and the negative words they spoke to one another. They wandered in the desert for forty years until that unbelieving generation had passed away.

When Joshua was leading the Israelites out against Jericho, God instructed them to remain silent to prevent them sinning against Him. He did not want them to murmur and grumble as their ancestors had done with Moses. Joshua told Israel to be quiet until he commanded them to shout with a great voice.

> "Now Joshua had commanded the people, saying, "You shall not shout or make any noise with your voice, nor shall a word proceed out of your mouth, until the day I say to you, 'Shout!' Then you shall shout." Joshua 6:10 (NKJV).

There were clear reasons for God saying they should remain silent until the manifestation of their blessings; firstly if they had conversed with one another, they would have allowed the bug of unbelief to spread like fire, if they could master their unbelief then victory was assured; secondly there was the possibility that the weak minded amongst them would have been influenced by the views of the majority resulting in defeat.

By keeping silent they could: a) hear God speak to them individually b) strengthen their faith c) reflect on what was ahead of them d) know what God expected of them and e) strategise how they would claim their victory. When it was time for the Israelites to speak Joshua told them to raise a great shout to deafen the voice of their enemies and to reduce the great wall of Jericho to rubble (Joshua 6:20).

When an angel of the Lord appeared to Zachariah to inform him that his barren wife, Elizabeth would bear a son, Zachariah doubted the word of God and asked for a sign. The angel replied that Zachariah will remain dumb until the manifestation and fulfilment of his blessing. The angel knew that unbelief would result in negative words being spoken, which will attract negative comments from others around him. Elizabeth later gave birth to a boy and on the day of his circumcision, Zachariah was consulted for the child's name. The minute Zachariah wrote the name John on a table; God opened his tongue and he began to speak, bless and praise the Lord. God held Zechariah's tongue so that when it was time for him to speak; he would only speak words approved by God (Luke 1: 5- 23; 57 -64).

Jesus Christ realised that unbelief did not allow the people of Nazareth to accept Him, His messages and His miracles. The people in His home country had taken Him for granted and were sceptical about His calling and anointing so they spoke out in unbelief. They refused to listen to Him (God's son) because of their myopic mindset. Jesus Christ responded by saying that a prophet is not without honour except in his hometown; as such He could not perform many miracles there contrary to His desire as they had squeezed the zeal out of Him (Matthew 13: 54-58). We must be careful not to speak out in unbelief as this hampers the move of God in our lives. **We must also be cautious not to provoke God to silence.**

Leads to Inability to Control One's Anger

You lose your blessings through your inability to hear God's voice when you are angry. God did not say we should not be angry but in our anger we should not sin. Cain refused to listen to God who cautioned him to control his anger, which ultimately led to his destruction. Be careful not to destroy what has taken you years to build. **Don't forget that God's eyes are upon the righteous and His ears are attentive to the words they speak either for good or bad.** Proverbs 25:15 says that by long forbearance and calmness of spirit is a judge or ruler persuaded and that softness of speech breaks down the most bone-like resistance. No matter how fierce a person appears to you, a soft response from you will distil a "volcanic eruption" from taking place.

Let your speech be gracious at all times — seasoned like a broth of stew with salt for taste and flavour so that you will answer those who speak to you soothingly (Colossians 4: 6). Ask God to control your anger so that your speech and utterances are not like water from a dripping tap but rather like olive oil that is used as a soothing balm. In Job 31:30, Job said during his trials he did not allow his mouth to sin, neither did he curse his enemies nor pray for their death rather he prayed that his enemies would see God's goodness in his life. David kept a muzzle on his tongue in the presence of his enemies and remained dumb because he was a man of wisdom.

"I said, "I will guard my ways, Lest I sin with my tongue; I will restrain my mouth with a muzzle, While the wicked are before me." I was mute with silence, I held my peace even from good; And my sorrow was stirred up. My heart was hot within me; While I was musing, the fire burned. Then I spoke with my tongue" Psalm 39:1-3 (NKJV).

People who get angry too easily and so often don't have time to hear what God is saying to them. If you are prone to anger fits or spells, ask the Holy Spirit to put a bridle on your mouth, also ask Him to make you longsuffering and patient more specifically towards those who have the habit of provoking you to violence. Cain reached rock bottom because he refused to take correction from God. God told Cain that if he did well, his offering and gifts would be accepted. He advised Cain to consider his attitude when giving sacrifices as He looked at the inward heart of a man when he brings his offering before Him. Cain refused to listen to God and chose not to build on his strengths. Instead he focused on his weaknesses and doubted his position and relationship with God.

Chapter 8: Obstacles & Consequences of Failing to Hear God's Voice

He allowed his anger to overrule his sense of reasoning which led to his demise. He also lost his peace (Genesis 4: 5-7).

- **There is Financial Wastage**

When you stop listening to God, you start embarking on financial ventures, which God has not sanctioned, resulting in financial loss. God will never lead you into financial ventures, which will result in financial wastage and bankruptcy. God is a God of finance and you definitely need Him in your finances.

A few years ago I embarked upon some financial transactions without seeking God's approval first. I had joined an organisation by reading their glossy prospectus without enquiring from God whether the deal was right for me or not. This organisation had promised that I would significantly increase my property portfolio within a given time. Not only did this promise not materialise, I lost my joining fee and later entered into protracted correspondence with them to leave their organisation. During this period I had also embarked on a venture of internet marketing with a so called "reputable" company. I saw the signs from God telling me not to enter into contract with this company but I ignored God's leading. I went ahead with this business to build me the "most enviable website" but the company defaulted. I lost a substantial amount of money in this transaction.

The consequences for me in not seeking God's direction were drastic, not only did I lose time, money and energy; my finances spiralled out of control and downwards. As if that was not enough, weeks after these incidents, I got a call from my Managing Agent telling me that one of my properties had been partially burnt down by faulty electrics and that the tenant in another property was refusing to pay the rent. It was like I was being punished for my disobedience. My sister nicely reminded me that the financial wastage that I was facing was a direct result of me not listening to God on where and how He wanted me to spend my finances. I ate a lot of humble pies in that year, as I had to rein in my finances.

For the next two years after these incidents, I took stock of my finances and became more accountable to God. I asked God to forgive my arrogance and pride in not seeking Him first. It was then that God began to bring other financial transactions I had entered into previously to my attention. As I went through my financial dealings, God began to show me areas where I could cut costs and make savings. I closed ventures where there were overlaps. I then began to use the savings to pay off the debts that I had accrued along the way.

I equally began to study the scriptures on finances evermore carefully, I quickly found out that *Proverbs 17:16 which states that "a fool and his money are soon departed"* held true and I realised that I only had myself to blame.

I pray that you will search the scriptures to find out what God is saying to you concerning your finances, so that you can be profitable.

There is Relationship and Marital Breakdown

When you fail to/stop listening to what God is saying to you in your relationships and/or marriage disaster looms. You will see your relationships grow strong when God is involved. God will teach you how to build your marriage, your children and relationships. Don't allow disaster to occur before you take stock of where you are. How is your family doing right now? Do you need God's input? If your answer is yes, then start listening to God, and He will tell you which way to walk.

When you fail to heed God's Word not to associate with certain people in your life who are leading you off-course, you suffer the consequences of your disobedience. An example that comes to mind was when I decided to become friends with certain people in my life. I knew deep down that God did not want me to associate with these people but I ignored His warnings and pressed ahead with my friendship with them. They eventually betrayed my confidence. By the time I finally listened to what God had to say about the whole matter, I had lost hope and confidence in people. It took me years to recover from their betrayal.

When I look back to those years objectively, I know that I only had myself to blame. I had really only become friends with these people because I had erroneously believed that I needed them in my life. I got my just desserts for disobeying God's clear instructions. When God tells you to be careful with those whom you share your confidence in, you must listen to Him.

God's People Lament

The Book of Lamentations is proof that when God's people reject His Word, Message and Instructions, disaster is sure to befall them. God discarded, abandoned and disowned His people – Israel for their disobedience; He cast them out of His sight until they served their punishment. They lost their identity and forgot who they were as they were carried into exile to Babylon where they remained for seventy years. God allowed Israel's enemies to walk all over them, misuse and mistreat them because He was fed up with their behaviour. The Israelites wept and lamented as they realised that it was too late for them to change their ways. God had repeatedly and patiently warned the Israelites to change their ways but His Word had fallen into deaf ears.

To lament means to express deep sorrow or grief over an irreparable loss. Have you ever heard a person cry out in despair when they have suffered personal loss? Lamenting connotes that there is no way out of the situation they have found themselves and that they have gravely misjudged God. People also lament when there is a sudden realisation that they have been abandoned, rejected and discarded by God for their disobedience.

When we arrogantly disobey God's clear Word, Message and Instructions to us, we are sure to lament afterwards. At one time or another we have cried out when God reproved us for our disobedience, we have then asked Him to forgive us, He often does, however when God is tired of warning us He responds in an appropriate manner. We must never get to the stage in our lives where God abandons us because He has had enough of us. May we never reach the stage where there is no way back from whence we have fallen!

"Your ears shall hear a word behind you, saying, "This is the way, walk in it," Whenever you turn to the right hand or to the left" Isaiah 30:21 (NKJV).

Chapter 8: Obstacles & Consequences of Failing to Hear God's Voice

I sincerely pray that you will truly take stock of where you are right now with God and make the necessary changes so that you can live a victorious life in Christ Jesus.

> *You should make it your goal even in trying times to seek the voice of God; Do not allow the cares of the world to sweep you away from Him.*

CHAPTER 9

The Importance of Hearing God's Voice

"It is important to hear God's voice so that you will know that which He expects you to know; you will have the strength and courage to travel the path He has destined for you take and you will have the willingness to keep the instructions He requires you to obey." —Kehinde Adesina

It is imperative that you hear God's voice in the midst of the many voices vying for your attention. You must distinguish His voice in order to live a fulfilling and successful life. He speaks to those who are quiet before Him; therefore focus your attention totally towards Him for He will not have it any other way. You may choose to blame your family, friends or foes for distracting you, but the truth is that no one can

> *You may have to incline your ears away from the many distractions facing you on a daily basis in order to receive a personal Word from God.*

debar you from hearing God speak unless you knowingly, intentionally or recklessly permit them to do so.

There are times God chooses to remain silent to test our faith, obedience and commitment. When you are accustomed to hearing His voice, you will not be afraid during these times of silence because you understand that God has something up His sleeves and is expecting you to wait for His leading. **It is importance to wait patiently for Him so that you can make the right decisions.** Those who do not have a close relationship with God panic when He is silent as they feel they have to do something to get Him to speak; even in His silence, God is still speaking.

> *If you want to hear God's voice clearly and you are uncertain, then remain in His presence until He changes this uncertainty. Often much can happen during this waiting for the Lord. Sometimes He changes pride into humility; doubt into faith and peace...*
>
> *-Corrie ten Boom*

The question then arises: "why do you need to hear God's voice', 'how can you recognise His voice when He speaks' and "how does God speak to us?"

Why should you hear God's Voice?

You need to hear God's voice for the following reasons:

- **To lead a victorious life** - *Raphael Simon said, "To fall in love with God is the greatest of all romances; To seek him, the greatest adventure; To find him, the greatest human achievement."*

- **To succeed in life** - Success comes by hearing and believing what God is saying to you about every area of your life. To succeed you must hear God in every step you take. Sometimes you are so in tune with God that you will hear Him tell you where to read for your exams. Whilst your colleagues are perspiring and crying in the exam hall, you will sail through smoothly. This is because you know something which they don't know!

On many occasions when studying for an exam in the past the Holy Spirit prompted me to read certain chapters of my book. I studied those chapters in detail and found out that the questions came from these chapters at the exam. In the early 1990s I started a course which I abandoned halfway through because I was not making progress in the exams. A decade later, a work colleague began to persuade me regularly to complete the course. I disregarded his advice. However, a few years later his words began to impress on my mind. I was persuaded that God had used this man to minister to me. I began to bargain with God, that if He really wanted me to complete the course, He will make me succeed at the exams at one sitting. The Exam Board agreed to re-activate my record and allowed me to continue from where I left off. I realised that God was having "His Hands" in this. I sat the exams and passed them with flying colours. I now know that the secret to my success was me hearkening to God's voice. By being sensitive to the Holy Spirit's voice I succeeded where I had previously failed.

- **To receive inspiration and clarity of Vision** - In John 5:30 we read that Jesus Christ did not only talk (pray) to the Father, He also listened to the Father to receive clarity of vision and purpose. Jesus said He only carried out actions after He had received His instructions from the Father. You must not only spend time praying (talking) to God, you must also spend time quietly in His presence listening to Him.

- **To have peace of mind** - satan tries to take peace away from the righteous through lies that he whispers in the inner recess of their minds. He allows the cares of the world to steal the peace of God's children. When you know what God is saying to you during those challenging times, your mind will be at rest.

- **To preserve your health and life** - We know the story of the young Prophet who died after eating food (see Chapter 8 of this book) and Elisha's young prophets who had eaten poisoned soup (2 Kings 4:40). We must listen to what God is saying to us about our health. *Proverbs 23:2 tells us that we should put a knife to our throat if we like too much food whilst vs 20-21 tells us not to give in to too much food or gluttony.* There have been times in my life when I have heard God say don't eat at particular restaurants because He knew that the food had not been prepared in a hygienic way but I disregarded His warnings and allowed the "lust of the eyes" to draw me into eating food that was detrimental to my health. I later ended up in the hospital with food poisoning where I uttered words of regret to all who had seen me cry out in pain.

If you have disregarded God's warnings in the past about your health or well-being resulting in your ill-health, return to God and He will return to you. Take care of yourself, slow down to rest, exercise and God will guide your path. *Exodus 15:26 says "If you diligently heed the voice of the LORD your God and do what is right in His sight, give ear to His commandments and keep all His statutes, He will put none of the diseases on you which He has brought on the Egyptians.."* Preserving your life could mean hearing from God about whether or not He wants you to embark on a certain voyage that is hazardous. *Proverbs 4:20-22 says "My son, give attention to my words; Incline your ear to my sayings. Do not let them depart from your eyes; Keep them in the midst of your heart; For they are life to those who find them, And health to all their flesh. (Amp)*

- **For creativity/ creative ideas** - Hearing God speak to you through His Word or others will cause your creative juices to flow. God is a God of creativity; He has endowed you with creative gifts and divine ideas which you can only discover and utilise fully when you move closer to Him. I have received ideas for a chapter or paragraph for books merely by asking God to give me creative ideas. I have also received an inspiration or creative idea simply by listening to the Bible on tape or iPod, from my Pastor whilst teaching or preaching from the pulpit or from other people whilst they were speaking. As God is flexible, He may choose to speak to you through your employer, employee, colleagues, friends, family and foes, the list is endless!

After completing the initial draft of this book, I gave a copy to my elder brother to read for his comments. Immediately upon receiving it, he asked me whether I had included personal testimonies about when I had heard God speak to me, I said no as I thought I had finished writing the script. Later that day, I prayed to God and asked Him to reveal to me the appropriate testimonies He wanted me to include in this book so that my book will be a testimony to others. I asked the Holy Spirit to guide me as I put the script away as I did not want to be influenced by my own reasoning or thoughts. A week later, as I got out of bed, testimonies which I had forgotten about began to come back to me, I quickly scribbled them down in my "ideas book" so that I could later incorporate them into the book.

- **His Word is the Source of your strength** - Our strength lies in God's Word. His word will give you the staying power to continue the race of life. You will not falter along the way during trying times; His Word will allow you pass the endurance test of life as He is the rock and strength of our life; He is the rock who gives us strength. God was the strength of Joshua's life. He gave Joshua the strength and courage to continue from where Moses had stopped.

- **To act promptly when He requires you to do so** - God expects us to act promptly when He gives us a word in season, if we don't do so, He would assign the task to another person to do it.

- **To prevent you from running ahead of God** - Isaiah 52:12.

- **To receive direction in life** - God states that you will hear a word behind you saying this is the way, walk in it, when you turn to the right and when you turn to the left. Without God's direction, we will miss the right path to take in life- Isaiah 30:21

- **To know God's plans** - We can stand in the gap of prayer for those near and afar off when God reveals His plans of destruction because of their sin- Genesis 18: 16-33.

- **To receive a fresh knowledge and revelation from God** - In Psalms 32:8, God says He will instruct you and teach you in the way that you should walk, He will counsel you with His eyes upon you.

- **To have a personal relationship and/ to fellowship with God** - The only way you can know the heart beat of God is when you daily hear what He is saying to you.

- **For discernment** - familiarity with God's voice will alert you to those trying to mimic His voice. You will readily know when God is not speaking to you.

- **To reveal other people's deception** - When Laban was cheating Jacob, God showed him what Laban was doing secretly; He revealed Laban's deception causing Jacob to take pre-emptive action (Genesis 30: 25-43).

- **To receive God's empowerment** - God speaks to us individually and collectively to empower us financially, spiritually, emotionally and mentally for the task ahead of us.

- To be assured of God's presence.

- To prevent you from falling into error or receiving false doctrine at this end times.

- To receive His blessings.

- To lead a balanced life.

- To receive confirmation of eternal life.

- To be refreshed.

- To receive enlightenment about your purpose.

How Can You Recognise God's Voice:

Some of the ways you can recognise God's voice are -

- By praying for the kingdom of God to become established in your heart

- By seeking Him daily you become familiar with His Voice

- By avoiding distractions during your quiet time with God
- By not grieving the Holy Spirit in your manner of living
- By being precise so that you can get a clear message
- By inclining your ears towards God
- By obedience to God's Word
- By meditating on God's Word
- By being expectant

How Does God Speaks to us:

God speaks to us through:

- Jesus Christ
- The Holy Spirit
- Scriptures
- Prayer
- Praise
- Worship
- Dreams
- Promptings of our hearts
- Angels
- Thunder
- Earthquake
- Stillness of His Voice
- You
- People
- Lightening
- Fire

Chapter 9: The Importance of Hearing God's Voice

- Wind
- Psalms
- Signs and wonders
- Proverbs
- Words of wisdom
- Word of knowledge
- Impressions
- Visions
- Prophecy

Testing the spirits (1 Thessalonians 5: 19 -24):-

You need to test the spirit behind every word given to determine whether the source of the word is from God or Not. In order to accurately test the source you need to determine the following:-

- Is the word given scriptural, i.e. does it accord with the Bible, if it doesn't, then it is demonic
- Is God's character displayed by the word given
- Does the giver of the word display or have the fruit of the spirit, if not, then the person is not led by the Holy Sprit as no good tree bears bad fruit, nor does a bad tree bear good fruit as each tree is recognized by its own fruit
- Is the giver of the word harbouring any sin
- Is anything tainting the word
- Has God confirmed the word that has been given to you? Personal prophecy given through another is usually a confirmation of what God has already said to you. You must be wary of accepting prophesies from others without asking God to confirm it.

The Holy Spirit will place a caution in your spirit when a prophecy is not from God Please note that for every genuine gift there is a counterfeit. You must check the source as the spirit of error also speaks. Matthew 24:3-4 states that we should take heed so that no one deceives us and leads us astray. On some occasions you may be putting up an unnecessary resistance to God's word. Always ask the Holy Spirit to enlighten you as He is not the author of confusion. You must not put out the Spirit's fire by your contempt of His prophesies as God's Prophesies will come to pass at the appointed time, as His Word never fails. Even when God uses others to speak to you, He will still confirm His Word to you. **His Word will be confirmed through the peace you have in your heart.** Once you receive the word given, you need to interpret the word accurately and not out of context, i.e. don't just take the word literally and act upon it to your detriment you must ask God what He saying in each given situation.

God has spoken to me through some of the above mentioned methods. On numerous occasions men of God have given me a word pertaining to my future; some of which have come to pass whilst others are yet to be fulfilled. On other occasions when studying the word of God or when listening to the word of God on CD I have heard God speak to me clearly about my situation.

Without hearing God's Voice, hurdles cannot be crossed, mountains cannot be climbed and destinies cannot be fulfilled. My hope is that you appreciate the importance of hearing God for yourself before the eyes become dim; the ears become deaf, the (body) dust returns to the ground from where it came from and the spirit returns to God who gave it.

Conclusion

It is evident that those who will live victoriously are those who heed God's voice and walk in His ways. God's word brings revelation and understanding to the undiscerning. Our spiritual maturity increases as we begin to hear God distinctively for ourselves. To succeed in life you must therefore incline your ears to God's Word to hear what His Spirit is saying to you. You must seek His voice like precious diamonds and gold. Expend all your God given hours to diligently seek Him and you will surely find Him.

> *He will hear you when you call out to Him.*

God will be gracious to you at the sound of your voice. When you don't know what to say or how to phrase your prayer, He still understands the yearnings and desires of your heart. God is merciful and gracious to those who call out to Him. He vindicates us when we are circled and encompassed around by the enemy. He always comes through for us.

Hearing God's voice will cause you to hear and see a new vision for your life, it will cause you to have a new heart to seek only God's will. You will live on a higher dimension than those around you as God will begin to converse with you on a personal level. You will only know what will take place in the future when you hear what the Spirit is saying to you (Revelation 4: 22).

You can only truly live a victorious and fulfilled life when you listen to the voice of God, and obey, trust and respect His Word.

Thanks so much for reading this book. I hope you enjoyed it and have now opened up your heart, mind and soul to hear the message that God intends for you to receive.

I pray that God's blessings, Grace and Spirit will be bestowed upon you.

If you have found this book helpful, kindly provide your reviews on the website you purchased a copy of this book from or the various publishing platforms such as Amazon, CreateSpace and Lulu.

Other Books by Author

Become All That God Has Created You To Be

The Beginners' Guide to Wealth Creation

A Simple Guide to UK Immigration

The Beginners' Guide to Writing, Self-Publishing and Marketing a Book (out July 2013)

Purpose2Destiny TK Limited

P O BOX 3162
Romford
RM3 9WR
United Kingdom

www.ingramcontent.com/pod-product-compliance
Lightning Source LLC
Chambersburg PA
CBHW071511040426
42444CB00008B/1591